C000230452

ISBN 978-0-266-20577-7
PIBN 10210267

THE BIBLE

AND

LAND.

"O Earth, Earth, Earth, hear the word of the Lord!"—*Jeremiah.*

BY

JAMES B. CONVERSE.

MORRISTOWN, TENN.
REV. JAMES B. CONVERSE, PUBLISHER.
1880.

4514

Mr J. C. Rowell

Yours truly

James B. [illegible]

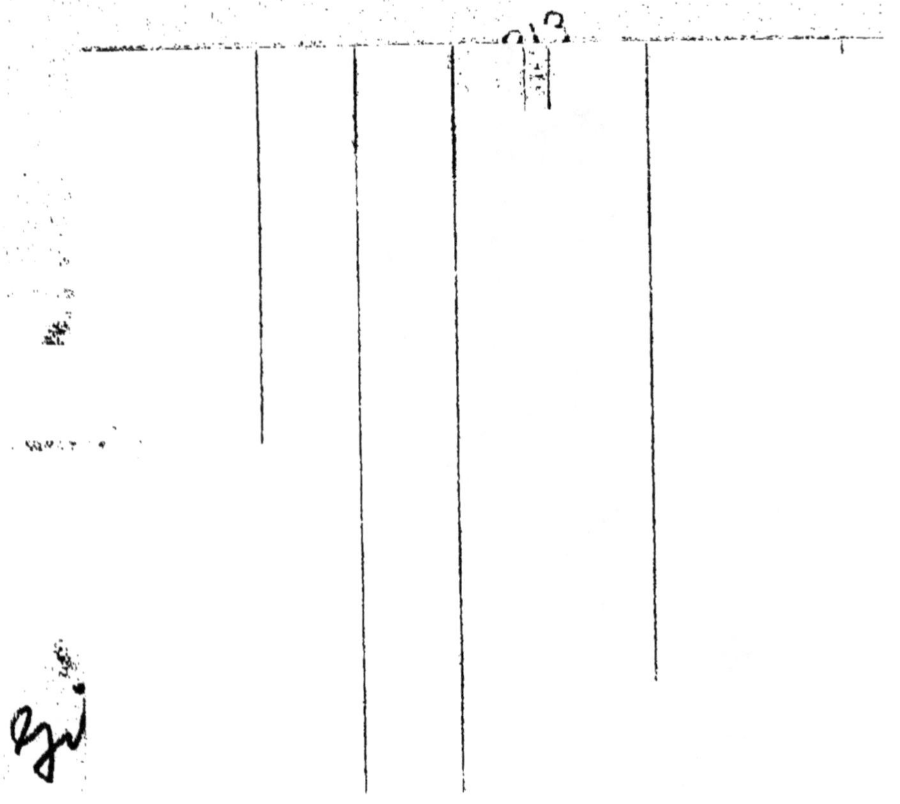

PREFACE.

The world is filled with books. The author, like the passenger who pushes into a crowded omnibus, feels like making an apology. My apology is an extract from an opinion of the Rev. J. M. Sherwood, D.D., the editor of the *Homiletic Review*, who examined the first draft of this book. He wrote:

"The manuscript itself is an extraordinary one. It does what George and other writers and theorists on the land-tenure question have failed to do—gone to the Bible, to the institutes of Moses and the legislation under the theocracy, to determine the matter. And I confess to a great surprise, he *establishes*, clear as sunlight, one of the fundamental points of George's theory, while he *routs*, *annihilates* another essential doctrine which he teaches, and which is the one of the greatest evil and danger.

"The argument is certainly an original one, and contrary, as a whole, to the received ideas, held and taught in our social science and political economy text-books. And yet it will and must commend itself to all fair minded, thinking people. I do believe it is an eminently timely little treatise (it will make but a small book), and that its publication would shed much light on a most perplexing subject, now before the public mind, and go far to guide the public sentiment to a wise decision in the matter."

Thanks are due to the Rev. James Park, D.D., of Knoxville, Tenn., for reading the proofs.

CONTENTS.

CHAPTER IV.

LAND VALUES.

CHAPTER V.

GROUNDS OF OWNERSHIP.

CHAPTER VI.

THE TERMS OF THE ORIGINAL GRANT.

CHAPTER VII.

BIBLICAL LAND GRANTS.

CHAPTER VIII.

THE LAND LAWS OF MOSES.

CHAPTER IX.

THE LAW OF THE TITHE.

CHAPTER X.

THE PROPHETS AND LAND.

CHAPTER XI.

THE BIBLE AND LIBERTY.

CHAPTER XII.

GOD'S GOVERNMENT AND GOD'S LAND.

CHAPTER XIII.

THE FUTURE OF EARTH.

INTRODUCTION.

This book demands that all taxation be imposed upon the value of land. It makes the demand in the name of the Creator. It asks it because such a mode of taxation alone is in accord with the Creator's plans, as made known to us in creation. It demands the single tax, because it is just and right. It demands that taxes be removed from poverty and imposed upon property.

This demand must not be confounded with Mr. Henry George's plea for the confiscation of rent. The two books, "Progress and Poverty" and "The Bible and Land," are unlike. The first is not theistic.* The second is intensely theistic. The first knows nothing of creation. The second is founded on creation. The first wishes to destroy the value of land. The second wishes to preserve and increase it. The first denies that land is rightly private

* We know little of Mr. George's religious views, except that he is not an infidel. We speak of the arguments of the book, and not of the author.

property. The second asserts that the title of the land owners is the strongest of all titles. The first asks the State to confiscate rent. The second shows that this would cause poverty and despotism. The first wishes taxation to be increased. The second labors for its reduction. There is not a single point of resemblance between the two books except that they both favor a tax on land. "Progress and Poverty" teaches that a land tax will abolish all poverty and destroy all greed. "The Bible and Land," while thinking that the single tax will greatly reduce poverty, confesses that only by the Gospel can the world be altogether reformed. In their premises, their arguments and their conclusions, the two books are thoroughly at variance.

For the convenience of the reader we subjoin a synopsis of the argument of the book:

The first chapter defines "Land,' claims it for God, and asserts that his ownership of land is the fundamental principle in political economy.

The second chapter states the great problem of our civilization, the growth of poverty with the growth of riches, and the increase of class distinctions. This tendency is illustrated by the present condition and past history of our country.

The third chapter, after defining the terms which we must use, enquires into the causes of the tendency of our industrial progress to produce poverty.

The fourth chapter refutes the economical portion of "Progress and Poverty."

The fifth chapter answers the ethical portion of the same book, and shows that the landowner's title to his land is indisputable.

The sixth chapter expounds the purpose of the Creator in the creation, which was that land should supply human needs.

As the Bible contains a statement of the principles of natural justice on which all human institutions should be founded, the seventh chapter gives an account of Biblical land grants.

The eighth chapter shows that in the opinion of the great Law-giver, as revealed to us in the Mosaic code, land is subject to special burdens.

The ninth chapter confirms the same truth by a consideration of the law of tithe.

The tenth chapter examines the prophecies

of the Old Testament, and shows that in God's judgment land is forfeited when not used aright. It also examines into the evils of excessive land holding, and investigates the economical causes of the sin of Sodom.

The eleventh chapter states the true theory of civil government.

The twelfth chapter applies to taxation the principles that have been established.

The thirteenth chapter is an inquiry into the future condition of the earth.

An appendix contains a reference to the texts of Scripture which throw light upon the land question.

CHAPTER I.

THE CREATOR'S TITLE TO LAND.

Definition of the word "Land"—The best Title to Property—God's Title—A Right Unrestricted except by Himself—Creation *ex nihilo* by Underived Power—The Fundamental Principle in Discussions about Land—Revolutionary—A Reasonable Demand—Politics and Piety—Natural Theology and Redemption—Natural Religion the Strength of Government—Creation, a Truth of Natural Religion, and a Fact in Political Economy.

God is the owner of all the land upon the globe. We use the word as a term of political economy. We mean by it the unartificial materials of industry. By it we mean the products of nature, out of which, or by means of which, man produces useful commodities. The soil, the ores in the earth, wild fruit, game, the sunshine that falls on the ground, waterpowers, etc., are "land," because from them labor produces wealth—food, clothing and tools. We use the word "land" to describe the whole class, because land is the most important of the unartificial materials out of which commodities are made, and also because they are all connected with the earth's surface. We assert that land belongs to the Creator.

The highest title to ownership is creation. What I make is mine. For this reason the word is commonly used as a synonym of earn. The employee "makes" his wages. The successful man makes his money. He gets a title to it by his labor. His title is good because he has worked for it. This feeling is instinctive, almost intuitive. We cannot question it. We can go no further back in the analysis of the question of *meum* and *tuum*, mine and thine. The race knows that it is wrong to steal, to convert the *tuum* into *meum*, without recompense. The distinction is one of those simple notions that are founded on eternal truths that need no argument; that are recognized as true, when recognized at all. And the strongest grounds on which proprietorship is founded, is that the thing made belongs to the maker.

For this reason, land belongs to the Creator. He made it; therefore it belongs to him, until he parts with his right to it. Unless he gives it away or sells it, it is his property. It is his to do with as he pleases. He can give it away unconditionally, or he can give it conditionally.

He can give it away for all time, or he can give it away for a limited time. He has a fee simple, a full, complete title. He can hold it himself or he can bestow it on others, on such terms, and for such periods, as he pleases.

God's right to the land is unrestricted and unlimited. We can manufacture wealth only out of pre-existing materials. We need wood to make furniture, wheat to make bread; cotton and wool to make clothing; iron ore to make tools; leather to make shoes, and we need soil and sunshine and rain to raise trees, wheat, cotton, sheep and cattle; and iron mines to yield iron ore. God created the land out of nothing. He spake and the world was. We only change the forms of matter; He made the matter itself.

In another respect God's title to the land is superior to all human rights. We can only work by derived power; He created by underived power. We can only labor by sustained power; He created by independent power. We are ourselves the product of creation; He is uncreated. We only labor as we receive the ability to labor from God; but God is the self existent. Human rights, even to the things that man makes, are therefore limited by the nature of his existence. The divine right to land is as unlimited as the divine nature. As the Self-existent, Underived and Independent, his right to the land, which he made, by his unaided and unsustained powers, is absolute and unqualified.

Let us go back in imagination to the time when there was no man to till the ground. Who then could dispute the Creator's title to land? At that time it was his, only and solely his. And it is his still, except so far as he has bestowed it upon others. The title that he had in the pre-Adamite age, he retains, except so far as he may have parted with it.

God's proprietorship in the land should be the fundamental principle in all land laws, in all the theories of political economies that treat of land, and in all social science that has to do with land. God's title to land is that on which all other titles must base, if they are just and righteous. The uses to which God would have his land devoted are the only purposes for which it can be righteously employed. Any other land titles cannot be defended in the court of pure justice and true equity. Any other employment of land than is allowed by the Creator is dishonest. Except so far as he has granted land, the title is solely in the Creator. His title still remains, unless a grant from him can be shown.

This assertion, in the present condition of law and political economy, is radical. The acceptance of it will revolutionize both sciences; for both practically ignore this great primal and fundamental fact. They do not deny it. They acknowledge in theory a Creator and a creation. They are both very pious on Sunday in church, and both quite atheistic in the legislative hall or the professorial chair. They acknowledge in their religious hours their indebtedness to God, and confess that all they have comes from him. But God's title to land is unrecognized, practically, in the laws and the theories about land. If Blackstone pays a passing compliment to the all bountiful Creator, if the coming of Christ or existence of God is recognized in the title of the bill, if the lecture on political economy is introduced with a prayer, or the treatise on political economy is embellished with a scriptural quotation, it is considered that the whole debt of law and political economy to the Creator has been fully paid. No reasonable man could ask more. Reasonable or unreasonable, this book demands more. It asks that God's ownership shall be practically recognized in land laws and land theories. It demands that land laws shall not be in opposition to the Creator's title to land. It requires that the theories of political economy about land shall accord with God's proprietorship.

Is not the request a reasonable one? Ought not laws to be in accordance with facts? Is not a law that is not suited to the circumstances of the people a bad law? So far as law is not in accord with the actual facts, is not the legislation imperfect? Adults have generally more judgment than minors, and a law giving the suffrage only to minors would be a bad law, because it was opposed to the facts. But it is not enough that legislation shall not oppose facts, it must also correspond with them. So far as it is not in accord with the truth it is imperfect. Law and justice, legislation and speaking the truth should be synonymous. It is impossible indeed that justice and law should always exactly coincide, and that the legislature should speak the whole truth in every case. For the law must work by general rules. It cannot take notice of exceptional cases. The legal precedent that does substantial justice in nine cases may work a great hardship in the tenth case. The law that declares truly what ought to be done in ninety-nine ordinary cases, may speak very falsely about the one-hundredth exceptional case. A perfect accord is impossible. But the land legislation of Christendom altogether ignores, and, indeed, in many respects is in direct opposition to, God's title to land. Is it not, to this extent, erroneous and faulty?

But it may be objected that God's ownership of land, while indeed indisputable, is a religions truth, and that legislation has and should have nothing to do with religion, except to protect the religious in their civil and political rights. As a truth of revelation, it lies without the province of the State.

The principle is admitted, but its application to the question is denied. The State should not establish any religion. Such an establishment does harm to the church that receives State patronage, and to religion itself. The conscience, as far as it relates to the spiritual, is beyond the authority of the civil magistrate. The State may not even express any opinion on purely religious subjects. And the Church should not express any judgment on political questions.* The two provinces, the spiritual and the political, are mutually independent. The province of morality lies between them, and owns a double sway; for the Church treats moral questions as they are related to God, and the State as they are related to man. The Church and the State have different aims; for while one seeks first the glory of God: the other aims first at the welfare of men.

This truth, that God is the owner of the land, is not such a religious truth as the State should ignore. It is not a doctrine of redemption.† It is not distinctively a doctrine of revelation. If Genesis had never been written men would know by reason that there was a creation. It belongs to that system of truth, commonly called natural theology, on which civil government is founded, and without which it could not exist. The name, natural theology, is ambiguous and unfortunate; but the distinction between natural and revealed theology is important. The State continually

*I earnestly hope that the truths contained in this book will never be preached from any pulpit, except as they affect individuals and personal conduct.

†Christ will hardly be named in this volume—another proof that its doctrines should not be preached from the pulpit, which is to preach Christ.

recognizes and acts on the truths of natural religion, made known by the conscience and the reason of mankind. They are everywhere and always known to be true. Among the doctrines of natural religion are such as these—that stealing, fraud, murder, and unchastity are wrong. The civil magistrate, accepting its teachings, punishes the robber, the forger, the murderer and the bigamist. Natural theology teaches that contracts should be kept; and the civil courts and laws about contracts are founded on this doctrine. The State revolves in the sphere of natural theology. If society makes a law opposed to it, contrary to the sense of right and justice that exists in the human breast, it is enforced with difficulty and constantly tends to become a dead letter. The strength of the State is drawn from natural religion. If her laws and regulations are felt to be unjust and unrighteous, she is to this extent weak. Her power is drawn from the approval of her people. She is constantly appealing to the judgment seat of God to secure truth from her witnesses and fidelity from her officers. Do away with the belief in God and in responsibility to God; and society must either be dissolved or become a despotism, ruling by brute force. When Rome lost faith in her gods she was ruled by her legions.

The truths about creation and the Creator belong to natural and not merely to revealed religion. They did not originate with the Bible. They do not prevail exclusively in Bible lands. They are undoubtedly explained and enforced by the Bible, but they are, and have been known without it. They are general truths, common to the race, like the other truths of natural theology, that there is a judgment to come, that stealing is wrong; on which civil order is founded, or about which the magistrate occupies himself. And no good reason can be alleged why legislation should ignore this truth.

Every truth has different faces, and the fact of creation looks toward the glory of God and the redemption of man. This aspect of creation the State may and should disregard. Her time is fully occupied in looking after the well-being of society. But creation also has a bearing on human legislation concerning land, and this can not safely be disregarded by lawmakers. God's ownership of land is the ground, the basis, of all other land titles, and this grand, fundamental fact should have an influence upon land legislation.

Political economy should also recognize this truth. It is a science, and science should admit all facts connected with it. If any science ignores any fundamental truth, it is to that extent faulty and erroneous. An astronomy that says nothing about the law of gravitation, a physiology that ignores the circulation of the blood, a psychology that knows nothing of intuitive truths, are imperfect. The more diligently they pursue their enquiries, the further they go astray. The more refined their speculations the deeper they sink in the mire. The more eloquent their reasonings, the more harm they do. Political economy is no exception among the sciences. The fundamental truth in all speculations about land is the proprietorship of the Creator. As the earth revolves about the sun, so must all speculations about land titles revolve about the ownership of God. As the sun holds the earth in its orbit, so must God's title to land govern all human titles. If the undevout astronomer is mad, what shall be said about the political economist who has never heard of the creation?

But what practical advantages, it may be asked, would come from the acknowledgement by law and political economy of the truth that the land belongs to the Creator? Generally, it may be answered, that all truth is useful, and that this truth is very important. A more detailed answer to this question will be found in the chapters that follow.

CHAPTER II.

THE PROBLEM.

Equality of the Savage State—Of a Primitive Agricultural Community, which is Destroyed by Industrial Progress—The Inequalities of the City—The Two Conditions of Equality and Inequality can still be observed—American Equality before the Civil War—Inequality in our age, the Result of Industrial Development—It is still growing—A Great Evil—The Curse of Riches—The Curse of Poverty—The Inequality a Social Danger—Discord—Different Laws for the Rich and the Poor—Can Liberty Exist with Inequality?

As industry develops, inequalities appear and increase. As the country increases in population and wealth, the class distinction between the rich and the poor, between "masters and servants," employers and those employed, between those who can live without working and those who work without living, becomes more marked and fixed. In a savage state (which however, we think was not the primitive condition of man) there is little inequality between the members of the tribe. All work or hunt, have the same knowledge of nature, fight with like weapons, work with like tools, dress in like material, eat like food and suffer the same privations. The differences are small. The chief's club may be more elaborately carved, his robe more embroidered, and his wigwam larger, but the inequalities are small. None have greater leisure, more knowledge, and much greater wealth than others. None can live without sharing the labors of the tribe; and none who share those labors fear that they will fare worse than their comrades.

In a primitive agricultural community, such as may still be found in the mountainous regions of the South, there is a similar equality in condition and in education. All the men are acquainted with the manly industries of the community, and all the women with the womanly arts. The men can all plough and reap, build a barn or a house, make or mend shoes and harness, wagons and rakes. The blacksmith is almost the only artizan, and the farmers, if they can borrow his forge, can shoe a horse or mend a plough. The women can all cook and preserve, card, spin, and weave the cloth and cut and make the homespun garments worn in the "cove." And the farmers share very much alike. They live in similar houses, and are engaged in like occupations, eat like food, and wear like clothes.

But when industry develops, differences appear, and with every step in material progress they increase. More trades appear. The mountain stream is set to work, and there are factory hands, who live a life unlike that of the surrounding farmers, and an employer, who works with his eyes and brain, instead of his hands. As population increases, land grows in value; and the owners of land have an easier time, and those who own no land have a harder time than they did before. The men work with better tools. The women are no longer constantly employed in spinning and weaving. The people have better shoes and clothing, better roads, better school-houses and churches, have a more varied diet. Much more of the products of labor come from the same amount of toil. But the old equality of condition has disappeared. Some have knowledge of which others are utterly ignorant. Some are now much better off than others. They have better clothing, richer food, finer vehicles, handsomer houses than the others have. There is now a class of employers and a class of hirelings. And as the industrial development goes on, the inequalities, once entirely unknown, tend to increase. The rich become richer and the poor poorer and more dependent. The children of the rich start where their fathers left off. They have a better education. In the community where once there were few inequalities, they are now marked. Where once there was only one class, there are now well defined classes. Where once all were equally independent, some are now dependant or others independent. One class lives without manual work, and the other class depends on the day's work for the day's bread. And this class distinction becomes more and more settled till at last, in old agricultural countries, (as in England,) the farm laborer is always on the verge of want. The wolf lurks near the door. The work of all the members of the family is needed to support it. When work and wages cease, the only alternatives are suffering or the poor-house.

In cities, where the industrial development is carried further, the difference is more clearly seen. Where one factory creates in a day more wealth than could be produced in a county in a year, the difference between the proprietor and the operatives is still more marked. The one lives in a palace that would buy a hundred farms; the other in a couple of rooms in a tenement without sunshine, almost without air, without the opportunities of privacy, and without much hope of bettering his condition. As cities grow, the avenues increase in splendor and the alleys in squalor. Millionaires and beggars multiply. Private carriages and tramps increase in number. The rich grow richer and the poor poorer. Capitalists seek new investments, and wage earners practice new economies. Many can live without work, and multitudes live only from hand to mouth. A day's holiday deprives the family of some comforts; a week's sickness endangers their home, and a month's enforced idleness sends them to the poor-house. The luxury of the one class and the anxieties of the other grow together. Money makes money and want increases want.

By two day's travel any American student of social problems can verify this statement. One day he may spend in any one of our large cities in contrasting palatial residences with tenement houses, in seeing the luxury of the rich and the misery of the poor. A day's travel in a Pullman car and another on horseback will bring him to the primitive community. In the whole neighborhood he will find no splendor and no beggary. Industrial progress has only commenced. The finest house in the valley is a log house with a stone chimney, and floor of rude planks; but all have log houses. The most luxurious food they have is bacon and greens, corn bread and strong coffee; but all, the observer will find, fare very much alike. The finest clothing is homespun and calico, but it is the poorest as well. The student need not fear to intrude, for he will be hospitably entertained in every house. The farmers have time to talk to him as long as he will stay. They never hesitate to take a day to listen to the political speaking, or a week to attend the camp meeting. For while none are rich all are independent. Although the results of labor are meager, the tools poor, the dress rude, the diet unvaried and the work hard, there are no paupers. The widows, the orphans and the confirmed invalids alone need to be helped. None are cultured, but all can think and talk intelligently on the subjects that have come under their limited observation. We do not say that this is a better social state than that of the city, where some are very rich and some are very poor, where the results of labor are much greater but are very unequally shared. But we simply call attention to the undoubted fact that in this primitive agricultural community there are not those class distinctions and those inequalities in fortune that are found in richer communities. Where there is no longer a contest with nature for existence, where the railroad destroys distance and the telegraph time, where steam and machinery multiply ten thousand times the productive powers of man, where the productions of the four quarters of the globe are found in stores on every square, where civilization has most advanced, the inequalities in condition are greatest. In the ruder community all are independent: in the more advanced community, multitudes hover over the abyss of want, shame and crime. In the primitive state of industry all share very much alike. Where industry has developed, the luxury of the rich and the privations of the poor keep pace with each other. The contrast between a primitive and an advanced stage of industry may still be observed in our country. In the next age it will not probably be as visible.

The effect of industrial progress can be seen by any middle-aged American citizen by looking back thirty years. Before our civil war there were few millionaires and no tramps.

There was much less wealth in the United States and much less want. There were indeed some rich and some poor; but the contrast was not so marked. There were few gentlemen who were not engaged in business of some kind, and few workmen who could not get work to do. There were fewer private carriages and fewer beggars in our cities. Servants in livery and women in rags were almost unknown. Few lived without work and nearly all who wished could earn good wages. Our wealth, in spite of the waste of our war, has vastly increased. Industry, invention, civilization, have progressed, and at each step the differences in society have increased. Before the war there was little of class distinctions, except in the South, and now these distinctions are marked and well settled, and tend to become stronger and greater.

No one can deny, it seems to us, that industrial development in our age and country has increased the inequalities of society. Our civilization has made the distinction between the poor and the rich. The rich are relatively richer, and the poor poorer. The rich may not be much more independent than the members of a rude and primitive society, but the poor are far more dependent. And the tendencies of the past are still in full operation. The laws that have governed our industrial progress are still in force. That which has caused these inequalities, whatever it may be is making them broader. We are marching in the old industrial road. There has been no change in the methods of our industrial progress.

Whether this is the necessary effect of the development of industry is an altogether different question. Is it an unavoidable result of material progress that society should be divided into distinct classes? Does invention always tend to make the rich richer and the poor more dependent? Is it of the essence of civilization to develop two classes, one that can live without work, and another that even hardly live by their work? These are questions that we do not now stop to answer.

This separation of society into the two classes of capitalists and operatives, wage earners and wage payers, of the rich, who can live on their incomes, and the poor, who can not drive the wolf from their doors, is a great social evil. It is harmful to both classes. The prayer of Agur—"Give me neither poverty nor riches"—is a good prayer for all men in all ages. It should be inscribed over the desk of the professor of political economy and over the chair of the president of the legislative body. The curse of riches is only equalled by the curse of poverty; and both riches and poverty curse the political society in which they prevail.

Riches that relieve their owner from the necessity of labor, injure him bodily and mentally, morally and religiously. It is a question whether perfect health can be maintained without regular bodily exertion. Athletic games do not take its place. Gymnastics strengthen the muscles, but do not lengthen life. Exercise, to produce its full benefit, must occupy the mind. Walking for exercise is not as beneficial as walking for an object. The mind needs still more the spur of enforced occupation. The soul that feeds on itself will soon consume itself. For this reason solitary confinement has proved to be such a severe and brutal punishment; for neither mind nor body have any occupation. But riches that deprive their possessor of the necessity of working, rob him of the greatest incentive to labor, and take from him also the great safeguards of virtue. Idle hours are the devil's gain; idle hands are his tools, and empty souls are his abode. Thus, bodily, intellectually and religiously, great riches curse their possessor. A moderate capital, that makes labor profitable, is a spur to exertion and a blessing to its owner but a large fortune will ruin almost any body. As the sun shining upon the fields after rain makes the crops grow, so capital stimulates labor; but as the sun shining with undiminished force week after week withers the crop, so great riches blight their owner's body, mind and soul.

But, it may be said, the rich may find or make employment for themselves. Released from the necessity of supporting themselves they may give themselves to politics or piety, to art or science, and thus do a work for the community which men without leisure could not do. Some do this, and deserve the greater praise, because they disregard the example of their class; but most spend their income in elegant leisure. They make a business of pleasure. Their greatest labor is to amuse themselves. We cannot blame them much. Labor is irksome. It is pleasanter to play than to work. The world's work has not been done by rich men of leisure. Its preachers, reformers, poets, artists, philosophers, statesmen, lawyers, inventors, have been, for the most part, men compelled to labor. The incentive to labor, the necessity for self-support, is needed by nearly all who have formed habits of industry. Most work best under the lash.

But when that lash is a Roman scourge loaded with balls that sink deep into flesh and nerves, it changes freemen into slaves. The fear of the poor-house is not a healthy stimulus to labor. Continual anxiety, lest when the work gives out, or the health fails, the children may starve, brutalizes the laborer. Poverty that dreads starvation is pernicious to body and soul, to health and virtue. It leads men to drown their fears in drink, to curse their Maker, or to steal. The howling of the wolf at the door drowns the voice of conscience. The toil that leaves no time for God, for reflection, for culture, for nothing except the fear of want, changes the toiler from a man or a woman into a machine. If men and women are the children of God, such toil is an impiety. If indeed, civilization, industrial progress and material development compel it (a proposition which we shall deny), then they are an evil and not a good.

The separation of society into the two classes of the very rich and the hopelessly poor is a menace to society. It endangers social order. We call society a commonwealth. It is a community. Some speak of it as an organism. We must not press the figure too far; for it is indeed a figure and not a fact. The growth of society resembles the growth of an organism in many respects. It almost seems as if people were members of society, as the arms are members of the body, or as believers are members of Christ. But it is certain that mutual sympathy is necessary to the prosperity of society. A regard for the common weal is necessary for the very existence of the commonwealth. But this separation of society into classes destroys social sympathy. The rich naturally sympathize with the rich, and the poor with the poor. Instead of one life in the society there are two. The society is no longer a community. Instead of unity there is diversity. Instead of peace there is civil war. One part of the society fails to sympathize with the other part. Instead of social concord there is discord, and to this extent the bonds of society are loosened.

This mutual sympathy of the rich for the rich, causes social injustice. There is one administration of law for the rich and another for the poor. If a poor man commits a crime he is rapidly tried and quickly condemned. If a rich man commits a crime the process of condemnation is long and tedious. The indictment is closely scrutinized. The jury is carefully empaneled. The witnesses are sharply cross-examined. There is a long debate as to the exact meaning of the law and the force of the testimony. There are appeals and motions and delays of every kind. There is practically one mode of trying the poor and another, far more deliberate and tedious, for trying the rich. And the property class have a greater influence in making the laws as well as in executing them. The laws make the sins against property greater felonies than the sins against humanity. Of course there is no deliberate intention to do this. Self interest blinds all, and the rich form the governing class.

Our republic was founded when the class distinctions were not so distinct and general. Can republicanism last when a part of the people are millionaires and another part beggars? Government by the people is possible when they are independent. Can it endure when three-fourths of the people depend for their bread upon the other fourth? Will our civilization destroy our liberties? Will invention and material progress destroy the framework of American society?

CHAPTER III.

THE CAUSES OF POVERTY.

The Apparent Cause of Poverty—Is it the Real Cause?—Definitions—Value—Utility—Rent—The Law of Rent—Labor and Laborer—Wealth—Capital—Wages—The Three Partners in Production—The Demands of Land must be met—Other Causes of Poverty—Sickness—Intemperance—The Division of Labor—Monopoly—Taxation—Extravagance—The Cure for Poverty is Christianity.

Industrial progress has apparently produced in our country the class distinction between the rich and the poor, capitalists and operators, wage earners and wage payers. And these distinctions are growing deeper and more marked. Thirty years have made a great difference in our country. In 1858 there was work for nearly all, and living without work for very few. In 1888 there is a large class that is supported without working, and a larger class that can hardly live by working. The end is not yet. The forces that have created riches and poverty are working with greater energy. The backwoods districts where land is very cheap, where there is neither luxury nor beggary, are rapidly disappearing. As land becomes more useful and more valuable, as the reaper supplants the cradle, the factory the hand loom, the railroad the dirt road, the telegraph the mail boy, the "commercial emporium" the cross roads store, equality disappears, and some are rich and others poor; some dress in silks and some in rags; some eat foreign delicacies and some go hungry. As material development goes on, the differences between the rich and the poor increase and become more permanent.

Is industrial progress indeed the cause of this separation of society into the rich and the poor? Does invention, while increasing enormously the fruits of toil, rob some toilers of bread? Is our civilization a car of juggernaut for the worshippers of mammon to ride over the hearts of workmen to the devil's paradise of idleness? Or, if invention, industrial progress, civilization are not the cause of our poverty, what is it that is creating want and dependence in the midst of prosperity? Why have we in America, tramps and able-bodied paupers? We had neither forty years ago. This is the question of questions for all American citizens. The social salvation of our country and the preservation of our liberties depend on our answering it aright.

Before trying to answer this question we will define a few terms that we will henceforth use only in a technical sense.

Value and utility, valuable and useful are loosely used interchangeably. We distinguish between them. Value refers to cost, utility to benefit. Value is selling price, utility is usefulness. Generally they exist together. Useful things are usually valuable. But often they are separated in fact, as they can always be separated in thought. Air and sunshine are useful, indeed indispensable, but they are not valuable. Water has great utility, but generally it has no value. And, on the other hand, diamonds have great value and little utility.

Land we have before defined as the surface of the earth and its natural products, the unartificial materials of labor. Rent is the annual value of land. As we shall use the word it means both less and more than in its common use. Rent usually includes also the annual value of the houses and barns, the fences, orchards and other improvements that are on the land. It includes both the hire of the natural surface of the earth and of the results of industry placed upon it. We exclude the latter in talking about rent. Again, in common speech no land owner receives rent from ground which he occupies himself. But in our definition the annual profit that comes to the landowner from the mere ground is rent. The farmer cultivating his own soil receives rent; that is, part of his profit comes from his possession of the soil and part from his work. He receives both rent as a land owner and wages as a laborer.

Competition creates rent. In a community where there is enough land for all, and where all the land is equally desirable, both in fertility and in location, there is no rent. But if some of the land is more fertile than the rest or is better located, an advantage from the greater fertility or better location comes to the owner or occupier of the better land; and this advantage we call rent. If the advantage comes from greater fertility and nearness to market it is agricultural rent, but if it comes from location in centres of manufactures or of commerce it is business rent. If only part of the land is used the rent will be governed by the advantage of the occupied land over the unused free land. Rent is a premium that comes from the use of more desirable land,

and the amount of the premium depends on the desirability of the land over the free land. This is what is meant by the "margin of cultivation." If there is as much land yielding thirty bushels of wheat to the acre as will supply all those who wish to raise wheat, then land that will yield only twenty bushels to the acre will not be cultivated. But if the population increases and the twenty bushel land is cultivated, the land that will yield thirty bushels to the acre will command a premium; and this premium is rent. If the owner leases it to others it will be paid him; and if he cultivates it himself he will still have it, for he will get more wheat for the same amount of labor than the owner of the poorer land gets. If the margin of cultivation is lowered to land producing fifteen bushels to the acre, the land producing twenty bushels will now secure a rent to its owner, whether he leases it or ploughs it himself. But the desirability of land does not depend exclusively on fertility. The value and rent of land are determined as much by location as by fertility. All have an attachment to their homes, and land near them is more valuable than remote lands. The merchant and the manufacturer desire land where they can sell more goods or manufacture more cheaply and sell their goods easier. Mines, water powers, springs, climate, even prospects and shade, influence the value of land, by making it more or less desirable than other lands.

Other terms which we use in a technical sense are labor and laborer. In the ordinary use of the word, labor is manual work; and laborers are manual workers paid by day's wages. We mean by labor human exertion put forth for the supply of human wants All who work to supply human needs are laborers. Labor as we use it is not limited to manual work. The superintendent of a factory, the wholesale and retail merchants (as far as their personal exertions supply human wants), the judge and the policeman preserving public order, the preacher, the lecturer, even the actor and the mountebank, are all, so far as they use the powers of mind and body to supply the necessities of mankind, laborers. In the other sex housewives, seamstresses, cooks, doctors, teachers, are laborers. But play is not work. The exertion I use merely to please myself is not labor. If the minister walks a mile to visit a sick man it is labor; but if he promenades it is not labor. Personal pleasure in this sense is.

not a human need. The boundaries between work and play are indefinite, as all should take a personal pleasure in their work; but the distinction is real and important.

Wealth is the result of labor exerted upon land. Two factors are needed to produce wealth—land and labor. Without the natural and unartificial materials, labor cannot produce wealth, and until these materials are worked up by labor into wheat, flour, shoes, hats, houses, fences, railroads and other useful commodities, they are not wealth. According to this definition, bonds, stocks, bank bills, notes, are not wealth, but merely the evidences of debt, of the right to claim wealth. Land also is excluded. It is and ought to be property, private property, but it is not a product of labor and so can not be wealth. Real estate is partly land and partly wealth. The unimproved ground is land, the improvements, the houses, stables, fences, roads, etc., are wealth. The owner of unimproved land may be rich, but he has no wealth.

The distinction between land and wealth is not fanciful. Both indeed have value and are property, but they agree in nothing else. Wealth is the result of labor; land is not.

Wealth can be destroyed, land endures. Wealth of every kind needs care and protection, land takes care of itself. Wealth decays, land continnes. Wealth needs to be renewed from time to time, land improves when left to itself.* Wealth is consumed, land is not. The amount of wealth can be indefinitely increased, the amount of land is fixed. A demand for any kind of wealth, for shoes or matches, for example, will increase the supply and at last reduce the price; a demand for land will increase the price. Clearness of thinking requires that they be distinguished.

Capital is that part of wealth that the owner uses to assist his own labor or the labor of others. That part of our goods that we use for production is our capital. The wealth from which we expect to derive a profit is our capital. The wealth used for work is capital, and that used for play, for personal gratification, is not capital. The carpet in the merchant's store is capital, but when placed on the parlor is not capital. Meat in the butcher's shop is capital, but on the dinner table is not capital.

* This is not true universally. An untilled, neglected farm, "goes down," and decreases in value. Part of the decrease is due to the decay of the improvements; but a part is due to the growth of weeds and bushes. But even a deserted farm would increase in value in a period of years if the population is increasing.

In trade the goods in the hands of the producer or his agents or representatives (the merchants) are capital; when they pass into the hands of the consumer they cease to be capital. The boundary between production and consumption divides the wealth that is capital from that which is not capital. A capitalist is one who uses his means in production. He may himself superintend a factory, or he may loan his wealth, or obligations representing it, to some one who will run the factory. So far as his wealth assists labor is the rich man a capitalist, and so far as his riches are invested in land is he a landlord.

Wages are that part of the result of labor which are assigned to the laborer as a reward for his exertion. Wages can only come from the fruit of labor. The laborer is usually paid in money, which is the representative of wealth; but he may be paid in goods. He receives a portion, and generally only a portion, of the results of his labor for his remuneration.

The lines between the three classes, landowners, laborers and capitalists, can not be drawn accurately. There is not one class of landlords, another of laborers and another of capitalists. If there were our free institutions could not last ten years. Most rich men are land-owners, capitalists and laborers. Most capitalists own land and perform labor. Most laborers have some capital, and not a few own land. The income of very many is made up from three sources, rent, the annual value of land; interest, the annual value of capital, and wages, the payment of labor. The American farmer has rent, the use and advantage of his tools, stock and other wealth, and wages. But although they are thus practically combined, it is absolutely necessary for clearness of reasoning, that they should be separated in thought.

Three factors are necessary to create our wealth. Three partners—land, labor, capital—work together to feed, clothe and house our people, and to supply them with the comforts and luxuries of life. Without land labor is impossible. Neither the farmer, the carpenter, the shoemaker, nor any other artisan can make anything without the materials supplied by nature. Until labor has been expended the products of nature will not supply human wants. The fields must be tilled, the woods felled, the cattle tended, before there can be wheat, fuel or meat. And without tools, that is, capital, the production will be slow and the results scanty. Our wealth, that is the things we want for food, clothing, etc., is produced not by either land, labor or capital separately, but by the co-operation of the three factors. And the things produced (wealth) must be and are divided between the three partners in the production. The share of land we call rent, the share of labor is wages, and the share of capital is interest. What either one gets will depend upon what the others receive. If either partner takes more, the other partners must receive less. The total product of land, labor and capital is all that can be divided between them. If interest is abolished, those who are mainly or merely capitalists will suffer. If wages are lowered, those who are mainly laborers must economize. If rent falls, those who are chiefly landlords must retrench. Fortunate indeed it is for us that, the separation of our society into these three classes is not rigid.

If on the other hand rent rises, wages and interest must fall. Land is the senior partner of our industrial firm. Rent does rise. Land is continually becoming more valuable, in every progressive community. Its power is absolute. We must have land. And that wages and interest do fall as rent rises is not a matter of theory with us. It is a plain matter of observation. Our country is a continent. We have room to watch the industrial development. In the west where land is low, wages and interest are high. In the east where land is high, wages and interest are lower. In England, where land is higher, wages and interest are still lower. From the price of land it is easy to judge what wages and interest will be. There are so many States, so many industrial communities in our continent that we do not run much risk of error in laying it down as a general rule, (to which there may be exceptions,) that, in progressive communities, as the value of land increases, and rent rises, wages and interest diminish. And as a population grows, land increases in value and rent rises.

According to Mr. Henry George this law of political economy is the chief cause of the growth of poverty and pauperism with the growth of civilization. And his remedy for it, is to abolish private property in land. If land ceases to be monopolized, he believes poverty will cease. His remedy we will examine in the next chapter. But granting all he claims it is still apparent that there are other causes of poverty.

One cause is sickness and death. A Robinson Crusoe in a desert island, if he should be ill, would suffer the greatest privations in spite of the fertility of land that could be had free of rent. If he had married and had died his widow and children would suffer unless they could labor. When health fails the laborer must suffer, even if wages get all the product, and rent and interest none. The poor we shall have with us always. When population is scanty, when all are independent, when all know the circumstances of each, the generosity of the neighbors will relieve the sick and enable them by timely help to again earn their own living. But when population is dense, and poverty abounds, the knowledge and the means are wanting to relieve such cases, and temporary sickness creates permanent destitution.

Another cause of poverty is intemperance. The nine hundred million dollars that are squandered every year in this country for intoxicating liquors would give nine hundred thousand people an income of a thousand a year. The expenditure is responsible for a large part of the poverty of our country. But the squandering of the money is the smallest part of the evil. The bodily, mental and moral effects are far more terrible. The drunkard's wife would wear rags and the drunkard's babies lack bread if there was no such thing as land value or rent. The poverty and misery caused by drink are not chargeable to the increase of rent. And the tendency to intemperance grows with population and increases with industrial progress. The one who labors in the din of the factory feels the need of stimulants more than the one who works in the open air. In the primitive community (to which we have referred so frequently) where none dread poverty and where all can take a day's rest when they please, there is not so much danger of intemperance as where commerce and industry drive the toilers to their work three hundred and ten days every year. The temptations also are greater in crowded populations.

The division of labor which our manufactures require affects very unfavorably the independence of the laborers. In a primitive state of industry every laborer can do every kind of labor that is done in the community. In the savage state, each brave can hunt, fish, build a wigwam, dig out a canoe, make bows and arrows or manufacture robes and moccasins. In the backwoods each farmer is a carpenter, a mason and a blacksmith; can mend a wagon or a saddle. In such a community the laborer is much more independent than in a community where each laborer can only do a single thing. The country blacksmith shoes a horse, mends a wagon and next a plough, and then a hoe. The operative in a city factory does the same thing over and over again, ten hours a day, and three hundred days a year. The gain of the division of labor is of course immense. Ten men each doing a single thing can do perhaps ten times as much as ten men each of whom does ten things, and do it a great deal better. And it is nobler too for each to work for all, and all to work for each than it is for each man to work for himself and by himself. But if the social machinery breaks down, the man who works for himself and who can do all that is done in his community, is better off than the man who has only learned a single branch of a single trade. In a deranged industrial condition the one is more independent than the other.

Another cause of poverty is monopoly. Many kinds of business are necessarily monopolies. Such are railroads, telegraphs, gas works, electric lighting, street cars and water-works. Competition in such cases is impossible. The street will only hold one line of rails. If there are rival railroads, telegraphs, gas-works, water-works, the result of the competition is that the public has to pay more instead of less, until the unnatural contest is ended by the consolidation of the rival companies. For one company can do all the work, and do it better and cheaper than two can; and when there is competition the public has to pay the cost of both lines and the expenses of both companies. But monopolies cause poverty. They charge what the traffic will bear. The people have to pay tribute to those who own the monopoly. The owners grow richer and those paying the tribute poorer.

Another cause of the growth of poverty is that the burden of taxation is placed upon consumption, that is upon labor. Most taxes are shifted from one to another till at last they fall upon the consumer. If the merchant has a privilege tax to pay, he will charge a higher profit, and his customers, the people, most of whom are poor, must pay it. The tariff duties are not paid by the importers, but by the consumers. If the importer advances the duty he expects a profit upon what he pays to the government as well as on the foreign cost of the goods. Every merchant gets a profit on the tax as well as on the cost; for the two are indistinguishable. And all these profits on the government tax have at last to be paid by the consumer, that is, since laborers constitute the bulk of our population, by the laborer. Our protection tariff also burdens labor by creating unnecessary monopolies. Our "Trusts" are the fruit of protection. Taxes on wealth also are taxes on labor. As wealth is the result of labor, the taxation of wealth is the taxation of labor. The government might exact a tax for every day's work spent in producing wealth, instead of waiting till the wealth has been produced and then taxing the wealth; but practically the result is the same; labor pays the tax. As capital is the tool of labor, the taxation of capital is the taxation of labor. It is immaterial to the farmer whether the government taxes him say five cents a day for the hundred days he uses his team and wagon or taxes him five dollars a year for the privilege of owning a team and wagon. In both cases his labor pays the tax. Even part of the taxes on real estate are shifted on labor. If houses are taxed, fewer houses are built, till house rent rises enough to repay the tax to the house builder, so that in an advancing community even this tax is paid by labor. The burden of taxation rests on those least able to sustain it.

Another cause of poverty is extravagance. The family that spends more than its income becomes poorer every year. All possible reforms will not alter this fact. And the temptations to extravagance increase year by year with the growth of our civilization. In the primitive agricultural community to which we have introduced the reader, where the men wear jeans and the women linsey, there is very little temptation to extravagance. The man who goes beyond the common standard of living is laughed at rather than admired. But when civilization has divided society into richer and poorer classes, every one aspires to the higher classes. Fashion is a goddess and style rules. And the temptation seems to grow more irresistible. Honesty and honor sometimes fail to resist it.*

*Why does it cost more to live in the city than in the country? Nearly everything is as high in the country as in the city. Some

All of these causes of poverty grow with our civilization. In an undeveloped industrial condition they are weak. With material progress they increase. The end cannot be seen. The value and rent of land increase. Access to land, the materials of labor, becomes more difficult and costly. Sickness is a greater burden. The temptations to intemperance are more numerous, and the tendencies towards it are stronger. The division of labor makes the laborers more dependent. The increase of manual skill makes the position of the unskilled laborer worse. All the modern inventions tend toward monopoly. Machinery drives out of business the small producers. As civilization advances the functions of the State are enlarged, and taxation increases. There are ever new and stronger temptations to extravagance. Civilization creates poverty, and with every advance it adds to it. No one can point where this increasing tendency will

things—dry goods, groceries, shoes, hats, &c., are higher. Country produce may be lower, but the retail buyer frequently has to pay city prices, if the city market is near. Ground rent of course costs more in the city; but house-rent for the same style of houses is as high in the country. The difference in the value and the rent of the land on which the house stands, will not account for the greater cost of living in the city. The explanation is that the style of living is different, that the country people live in cheaper houses, wear plainer clothes, and have less variety in their food.

cease. The larger the population the more helpless is sickness; the greater is the burden of taxation. The more machinery, the greater will be the division of labor, the less is the demand for unskilled labor, the fewer shops and the more factories. Inventors have again and again hoped that their wonderful inventions would destroy want—only to be disappointed. The cheaper and handsomer goods are made, the greater the temptation to live beyond our means.

These are some of the causes of the growth of poverty amid the growth of wealth, which is the great peril of our time. The removal of one of them will be an insufficient remedy. If the effect is to disappear, all of its causes must be destroyed. Civilization, material progress, invention, will not destroy poverty—they rather increase it. The only thing that can establish the kingdom of heaven on earth is Christianity.

CHAPTER IV.

LAND VALUES.

A Deserved Compliment to "Progress and Poverty"—Its Theory as to the Cause of Poverty—Its Proposed Remedy—The Laws of Society, the Laws of God—The Law of Land Value—The Reason for it—The Law of Value—Illustrations of it—The Law Applies to Land—A Land Panic—Its Effects on the Woods—On Farms—On Mining Lands—On City Lots—Final Results—Illustrations—The Confiscation of Rent—First Result, Political Corruption—Second Result, Despotism—Third Result, Taxing the Poor for the Benefit of the Rich—Fourth Result, Vast Growth of Poverty.

Two years ago I read a book that absorbed me for weeks. The author's warm sympathy for poverty aroused interest; which his own faith in his science increased. His prophecy that his teachings will abolish want, ignorance, selfishness and greed, and purify politics fascinated me for a time. The eloquence of the style, the clearness of the arguments, the earnestness of the purpose, the strangeness of the conclusion, and the confident dogmatism with which it is asserted, all combine to make "Progress and Poverty" a remarkable book. Its author, alone among political economists, has reached the masses. His newspaper has a large circulation. He had a large vote for Mayor of New York. There are many good reasons for the success of the book. I desire to acknowledge my own indebtedness to Mr. Henry George. Except for his book mine would never have been written. And yet his conclusion is pernicious. His assertions about the rightfulness of the private ownership of land will be completely refuted and disproved in the next chapter. In this chapter we discuss his remedy for poverty, which is the annihilation of land values, and the destruction of rent.

The outline of his argument is given in the last chapter. In civilization there are three factors in production; land, labor and capital. Three partners are engaged in making wealth; and what they produce is divided between them. What goes to land is called rent. What labor gets is called wages. The part of capital is interest. These three, the land owner, the laborer and the capitalist, must combine in order to produce useful commodities cheaply and abundantly. In the savage state indeed, there are only two partners, land and labor; but without capital, wealth is produced very slowly. The wages of the laborer and the interest of the capitalist depend upon what rent land demands. Land demands more and more, leaving less and less for labor and capital, as civilization advances. All new inventions by which production is promoted, all new improvements in the arts and sciences, all governmental reforms, increase rent, which absorbs more and more of the profits of labor and capital, until the limit is reached where labor and capital will not reproduce themselves. For there is such a point. The wages may be so low that laborers will diminish in numbers. Interest may fall so low that men, instead of saving their wealth to use it as capital, will spend it in personal gratification. All above this point will be taken by land as rent. If the standard of living among laborers falls, their economy will enrich not themselves but their landlords. If they as a class become more industrious or more temperate or more intelligent, the advantages of their industry, temperance and intelligence will, in the course of time, go to the landlord. If capital is content with smaller interest, this benefit also will inure to the landlord. As population increases, as all the land is monopolized, as land values rise, more and more is seized as rent, and less and less is left for wages and interest. Labor and capital are natural allies; and rent is the enemy both of wages and of interest. Such, as I understand it, is the premise that is eloquently stated in "Progress and Poverty." It would be easy to make long quotations, but I have thought that I could give the argument more briefly in my own language.

If such is the cause of the poverty of civilization, the remedy is very easily perceived. Shoot the landlord. Destroy the value of land. Abolish rent. I would not represent Mr. George as advocating any agrarian outrage. But his plan is, since rent wants more than its due, not to pay any rent at all to the land owner, but have the State take it all in taxation for public purposes. He would thus abolish land values. He would leave to the land owner enough only to pay him for the trouble of collecting it and handing it over to the State. And such taxation would undoubtedly destroy land values. When dividends cease the stock is worthless. When the State confiscates the rent, land will be valueless.

The remedy is radical. But is it safe? To hang or behead a man would undoubtedly cure his toothache. But it is altogether doubtful whether the destruction of land values would at all remove the poverty of civilization, and it is positively certain that the confiscation of rent by the State would vastly increase both the breadth and the depth of poverty.

The laws of society which we call political economy, like the laws of nature, are the laws of God. I have however very little respect for the science of political economy as it now exists. It is narrow minded. It looks only at selfishness. Self interest is the only principle of human nature which it recognizes. But this is the lowest and almost the weakest of the principles that govern human conduct and human society.* But the doctrines of true political economy, like the doctrines of true physical science, are the laws of the Creator and the only modes in which his creation can exist.

One of these laws of society is that as pop-

* A friendly critic thinks that self interest is a "tolerably strong" motive for human conduct. But I have not changed the language. Life is dearer to man than anything else; and yet men have died for love, for country, for truth and for error, and even for "honor" to avoid the imputation of fear. Many motives are stronger than self interest, and govern mankind more than it does. If "self interest" were as strong a motive as political economy makes it, all would live healthfully, morally and religiously.

ulation and wealth increase land values arise. It has been so in every country on the globe. In barbarous and savage ages land has been nearly valueless. When civil order has prevailed, agriculture has flourished, manufactures have prospered and commerce has extended, land has become valuable. When civilization has decayed and cities have been depopulated, land has become less valuable. This is a universal law of all society. It is dangerous to trifle with law. Gravitation is a law of nature, and the architect who should disregard it and try to build in opposition to it, would produce a ruin. The political economist who tries to erect a social structure in opposition to a primary and universal law of society will do far more harm.

The reason of this general law is easily seen. What is both useful and also limited in amount needs the protection of value.* Without such protection it will be wasted and destroyed. Air is useful, but as it is practically unlimited in amount it does not need the protection of

* The reader must keep in mind during this discussion the distinction between value and utility. As useful things are generally valuable this may require careful attention. Mr. George's object is to separate them in the case of land, and to increase the usefulness of land by destroying its value.

value. Sunshine is essential to life but it is valueless because unlimited in amount. Water is usually valueless because it is so abundant; but if it becomes scarce it should be protected by value; otherwise the people will more quickly die of thirst. Illustrations of this law can easily be imagined. Suppose the value of broadcloth removed:—the first result no doubt would be that every one would have a broadcloth suit; but the second result would be that broadcloths would be spread as carpets, made into grain sacks or torn up into rags, unless the supply was unlimited. Since none could be got for money, none could be obtained for love. Suppose the price of silk reduced to one cent a yard:—every woman might have one or ten silk dresses, but after awhile no silk would be left. If the price of wheat and flour were destroyed, it would be used to feed cattle or fires, in preference to things that cost money. If, to suppose a case analogous to Mr. George's proposal, the value of orchards was destroyed by imposing upon the owners of orchards a tax that would nearly consume the profits of orchards, the result would be that no more orchards would be planted; that the existing orchards would be cut down (except what were needed to supply the personal and private wants of their owner), and the supply of fruit would be greatly diminished. And the State could not prevent this wasting, except by barbarous cruelty and stern despotism. The State can punish theft, but what has no value can not be stolen. The State can forbid one citizen injuring the property of another; but what has no value is not property. So that the prudent man who wishes to preserve a store of valueless food* to feed his family in the future, could not be protected by a civilized government. His only hope would be to conceal it. If discovered the finder would waste it. Such hidden stores would not preserve the race a year. The destruction of the law of value would dissolve society into chaos.

The removal of value from things that are both useful and limited in amount would destroy all commerce and stop all production, except for the personal wants of the producer. Unless they could sell or exchange it the farmer would not raise wheat, the hatter make hats or the weaver cloth, except to supply themselves with food or clothing. If food cost nothing, London and New York could buy

* The reader will please reread the last note, and remember, if "valueless food" seem a strange expression to him, that we are trying to comprehend Mr. George's idea of valueless land.

none, and their only hope of keeping from starvation would be the world's charity. It would be difficult for charity to help them; for if food had no value it would not be property and could not be stolen; and justice could not protect it while it was carried to the starving citizens. In a "fool's paradise" all things are grotesque and absurd.

Illustrations could be multiplied indefinitely. If medicine cost nothing and doctors charged nothing, every one who had a cold or sore finger would send for a physician, and those really sick would have more trouble to get one. If legal costs and lawyer's fees were abolished, the court dockets would be crowded with trivial cases. Diamonds are durable, but if they were valueless it would be harder for those wishing diamonds to supply themselves than it is now. If gas* were as cheap as water it would be used to cook, to drive engines, to heat houses, till little would remain to give light. If street cars were free, they would be crowded with those riding for amusement, and the tired workingman would find it harder to get a seat. What is useful and is limited in amount must have value to serve its true end.

*Some of these illustrations are taken from Mr. George. They show that he has not studied the law of value.

All have suffered by this law, that useful things that are limited in amount must have value. It is not likely that this book will ever fall into the hands of any adult who has not gone without some of the comforts or luxuries of life because he could not or would not pay the price asked for them. To the poor it sometimes seems a harsh unfeeling monster. And yet it is a beneficient law. Without it society would be anarchy, when the strong would seize and destroy all they wished, and the weak would want.

Land is no exception to this law. Unlike wealth indeed it can not be destroyed. But its utility can be destroyed. It can be recklessly used. Its fertility can be wasted. It can be ravaged.

Land is useful—indispensable. Without it labor is impossible. But in thickly settled countries it is limited in amount. In order that it may be wisely and carefully used it must have value. If land values are destroyed, which the confiscation of rent will do, the land will be abused wherever and whenever its wasting will yield a temporary profit.

Mr. George's plan for destroying land value will make the wasting of land still more certain. Not only is the value to be nearly destroyed but a fine is to be imposed for the holding of land. Every year nearly the full rent must be paid to the government. All land owners who can not pay the State the rent must sell at some price, at any price. There will be a never ending land panic. It will always be easier to buy land than anything else and harder to hold it; for, while every other kind of property is free from taxation, every year, a heavy fine, nearly the entire rent, will be imposed upon the owner of land. Under this plan nature will be always abused.

Take the woods for example. Our forests have a beneficial effect upon our climate. They mitigate the drought and delay the blizzard. Even now, when unimproved land has value and is lightly taxed, their rapid diminution causes alarm. Statesmen are discussing the question of their preservation. Legislatures are debating forest laws. No one who has seen the effect produced by one steam sawmill on the waters of a branch, in increasing the winter floods and diminishing the summer current, can doubt the importance of preserving our forests. But when land owners have yearly to pay to the State a heavy fine whether their lands produce a profit or not, when the buying and selling price of land is next to nothing, the trees will be felled as rapidly as the lumber, fuel, bark, charcoal, or ashes will pay for the work. The dreary hillsides will be left to lie utterly waste till nature can recover from the blow, while the springs fail, and the water hardly covers the river bed in the summer drought, but carries destruction in the spring torrent. Or, if to avoid this danger, the government exempts woodland from taxation, land-owners, to save their property, will let their meadows and fields grow up in woods, till there is an unwholesome growth of forests and the supply of food is diminished.

All farming lands will suffer. Cheap land has been the enemy to thorough cultivation in our country. Our soil, east and west, north and south, has suffered because land has been so cheap and abundant. The result when the selling price of land has almost disappeared, and the owner has annually to pay a heavy fine for holding land is one which no American farmer will anticipate with pleasure. From the past we can judge of the future. Where land has been worth only a few dollars an acre the aim of the American farmer has been to get the largest return in the quickest time and to move to fresher and cheaper soil. The wheat lands of Western New York were abused because there were cheap lands in Ohio. Illinois has likewise impaired Indiana, and Kansas, Missouri. Our farmers have ravaged our soil because land was cheap. What then will be the result when agricultural land is nearly valueless? The mode selected to destroy land value will hasten the result. If land costs fifty-cents an acre, and the government taxes it two dollars a year for rent (any similar figures will do as well) the farmer will have the stronger motive to abuse the land for the sake of quick profits. Or, is it proposed that the government shall prescribe the mode of cultivation and compel the farmer to adhere to it? This is the only way that rented land can be kept in good condition. Only a tyrannical, despotic government could make and enforce such regulations. What jury of farmers would convict a fellow farmer for not complying with a despotic and expensive requirement? The farmers would try to get as much as they could as quickly as they could without any regard to the soil, and hope to buy cheap land on which to repeat the same work of desolation. Good farmers would be forced by competition or led by example into the general practice.

In the new regime, the small farmers, the backbone of American society, would disappear. For, in order to destroy land values, the state rent must be very nearly a rack rent, nearly the full annual value of the land. A merely nominal rent will not answer the purpose of giving labor free access to land. But it is cheaper to fence large fields than small ones, to plough with steam than with horses, and to reap with the self binder. The small farmer, using the more expensive modes of cultivation, can not compete with the larger farmers in paying rent to the State. Every year more small farmers will relinquish the effort to pay the state rent, and become farm hands and their boys tramps.

Mining lands will be similarly abused. Much mining land will be offered for sale at merely nominal figures, but the State will annually exact a heavy fine for holding such land. Can any one doubt the result? The mining company will try to get the most coal or iron in the shortest time and cheapest manner, and then surrender the land to repeat the extravagant waste of natural resources in fresh fields. Even now when mining land is valuable, and no fine is exacted for slow and deliberate improvements, accidents are not uncommon; and what shall we expect when the value of mining lands has disappeared? When the mines have been thus hastily worked over and abandoued, coal and iron will be dearer.

Vacant lots in our cities would also be misused. Their proper use is to furnish sites for houses. When the value of these lands have been destroyed by the confiscation of rent, they will be occupied as pleasure grounds and parks for the rich. The merchants and manufacturers, when they find that they can secure lawns and gardens without reducing their capital, by merely paying rent to the State, will quickly occupy them. It will be still harder for the workingman to secure a home of his own convenient to business. The tenement houses will increase and multiply.

When land values have been destroyed by the State (for society could destroy land values as Mr. George proposes), there might be flush times for awhile. When natural laws are suspended no one can foretell the immediate result; and no one can tell the first result when the laws of society are suspended. But as the suspension of the law of gravitation would result ultimately in the dissolution of the globe, so the suspension of the law of land value would result at last in the desolation of our country. The soil would be exhausted under a system that offers great premiums for its misuse and none for its care. After the law of land value had been suffered to resume its sway (for the suspension of this law could only be temporary), nature would recover slowly from the blows inflicted upon her, while successive generations mourned and suffered because of the folly of their ancestors.

Land is the store-house from which labor takes the materials it converts into wealth. Its resources are not infinite, but limited. In old times it was the custom to give the city that had stubbornly resisted to pillage when it was captured. For a time the law of value yielded to force. The most costly articles were valueless. The soldiers took what they pleased without payment. Far more was destroyed than was carried off. The destruction of land value will give land to pillage. Our woods, our farms, our mines will be wasted. Much more will be destroyed than will be used.

The gain will be slight and transient, the loss great and enduring. It would be much easier to rebuild the pillaged city than to restore a desolated land to fertility.

Or land may be called the tool by means of which labor makes wealth. Let us suppose a law that American carpenters should pay nothing or very little for their tools, but should pay the State fifty cents a day for every day they used them. How long would tools last? The law would be like a law that land should cost very little, but a heavy annual tax should be paid for its use. Tools may be replaced; but land can be restored very slowly.

Let us have another illustration. In order to encourage American manufactures suppose the government should pay a bounty of five thousand dollars to the locomotive builders for each locomotive they built, and then, in order to raise the money to pay the bounty, a tax should be imposed on the railroad compauies of one hundred dollars a month for each locomotive used by them. This plan of encouraging home industry would be no more absurd than some we have. The result would be that after a few years locomotives would cost little or nothing, but the tax on each locomotive in use would be twelve hundred dollars a year. How much money, under such conditions, would be spent in repairing locomotives? Would not such a law be analogous to the plan of making land cheap while collecting rent for its use?

Land is the factory by which labor produces wealth. When the factory is damaged, the work must cease or go on in ruder ways with less results. The new political economy gives all its premiums for the reckless use of the machinery. It is like a government that should proclaim that every manufacturer might have a new factory for little or nothing whenever he pleased, but must pay a thousand dollars a month for using the factory. Would not each manufacturer try to wear out his factory and get a new one as soon as possible? Nature repairs the injuries done to her very slowly. It is better to pay a high price rather than injure the land.

Pernicious as is Mr. George's end, (the destruction of land value, so that labor may have free access to land) the means he would employ to secure that end are equally destructive. His proposal is to abolish all taxes except the tax on land (mere land without improvements), and increase this tax till it nearly equals the rent of the land. In order to expend the money he would have the government pay off the public debts, purchase and operate all railroads, telegraphs, gas and water works, etc., "establish public baths, museums, "libraries, gardens, lecture rooms, music and "dancing halls, theatres, universities, techni-"cal schools, shooting galleries, gymnasiums, "etc." In other words, rent is to be confiscated by the government although it does not need the vast revenue, and to be spent or squandered by it. The value of the rent of the land in the United States has not been computed. The rent of New York City is probably over one hundred millions of dollars annually. But however great the sum, it is to be taken by the State for the purpose of destroying the value of land.

The first result of confiscation of rent by the State would be, in our country, political corruption, boundless corruption, such as the world has never seen. To lay all taxes absolutely needed by government on land (not real estate; when we speak of land we do not include houses) would purify politics. It would simplify government. It would greatly reduce governmental expenses. It would abolish custom house frauds and perjuries. It would end the deceit and falsehood connected with the taxes on personal property. It would not in the end reduce the value of land. It would interest hereditary riches in politics, and bring into the service of the public the time and talent now squandered in pleasure and fashion. But the confiscation of rent would corrupt politics. Every year the government would have to spend a vast sum, the amount of which is yet uncomputed, not because it is needed, not because it can be wisely expended, but simply and solely because it has to be spent in order to destroy the value of land. A surplus at Washington has produced great corruption, but the confiscation of rent will create a greater surplus, not alone in Washington, but in the capital of every state, in every county and in every city. "Wheresoever the carcass is, there will the eagles be gathered together." On the carcass of American liberty and prosperity, all the unclean birds will sit and gorge themselves.

The second result of the confiscation of rent will be such a despotism as the world has not seen since the days of Rome. The people will no longer be freeholders, but merely tenants; tenants at will, tenants from whom it is proposed to exact nearly a rack rent. The State will be the worst possible landlord. The millionaire, the wholesale and retail merchant, the mechanic and the farmer will alike hate and detest their landlord. For the government must work by general rules. It knows nothing of special cases, sickness and death, bad seasons and dull trade. It can make no allowances. It can admit no excuses. If it did it would have little revenue, for all would pay in excuses instead of money. Death and taxes are sure. The State has the power to exact prompt payment and it cannot discriminate. It must be a harsh, relentless landlord. An individual may be a good landlord; the State must be a bad one. The agent of an Irish nobleman has an unpleasant task when he collects the rents after a bad season. But more unpleasant and more dangerous will be the work of the American sheriff who goes, after the best of harvests, to collect of the American farmer one-half, one-third, one-fourth, or even one-fifth of his crop, to be spent in maintaining public "dance houses" and "theatres." Such a sheriff would not be re-elected. No one could be elected sheriff who would consent to assist in the confiscation of rent. Only despotism, a military despotism, could confiscate rent. If the confiscation of rent were begun under free institutions it would necessarily change the government into a military despotism. Such a tax could only be collected at the point of the bayonet. Forts and garrisons must overawe the people. The tax collectors would often need their assistance. This is not theory. Rome had vast public domains. Pharaoh received rent from Egypt, and ruled the Egyptians with a rod of iron. The government of India receives a rent tax from the larger part of India, and rules it, perhaps justly, but by force. To whom the land belongs to them belongs power and authority. When the government virtually siezes the land by confiscating the rent, it necessarily usurps despotic power over the people.

The third result of confiscating rent is that the poor would be taxed more heavily than ever before for the benefit of the rich. The removal of all indirect taxes and of all taxes on wealth would be a blessing to all and especially to laborers. But it is not necessary to confiscate rent to do this. The necessary expenses of government can be paid by a land tax (and by a tax on monopolies) without destroying land values. Free trade, governmental reforms, a better railroad and telegraph service and the free museums, libraries, etc., etc., would all increase the State rent-tax which the poor would have to pay.* The supply of heat, gas and motive power as cheaply as water is now furnished, would raise the rent-tax. All these improvements and any others which a vivid fancy can depict, would make the city a more desirable place of residence, increase the number of those wishing to live in it and raise the rent-tax to be paid in part by the city poor. But these improvements, though provided at the public expense, would inure mainly to the benefit of the richer classes. The public museums, libraries, universities, technical schools, etc., etc., would be used chiefly by the well-to-do, by those having leisure. Day-laborers would have little time to frequent them. And as calico shrinks from silk, fustian from broadcloth, after the richer classes had taken possession of these museums, etc., the poor people would have little inclination to frequent them. We see this tendency in the church and college. The poor will not go to a church frequented by the rich,

* Some poor people, especially in the country, are land owners.

although the seats are free. Our richer classes have taken possession of our oldest colleges, Princeton, Yale and Harvard, and, although the charges for tuition are no higher than formerly, poor boys do not attend them. The improved railroad and telegraph facilities, paid for by the public, would be chiefly used by the richer classes. The cheap gas, heat and motive power, furnished at the public expense, would make their way very quickly into the mansions on the avenues; very slowly into the tenement houses, and not at all into the homes of the farmers. The latter indeed would have the added hardship of absentee landlordism. For the public revenues, as heretofore, would be largely spent in the cities and towns. Every year nearly the full rent would be carried off from the farmers who need it, to be squandered in the cities by governmental officers. The confiscation of rent would especially curse the poor, the very class it is intended to benefit.

The fourth result of confiscating rent would be the vast, almost illimitable, growth of poverty. The people need the rent themselves. They can use it better and more wisely than the government can. How many there are both in town and country who are kept from the poor-house by the possession of a home, a garden, or two or three small fields! Deprive them of a large part of these advantages by a rent-tax and the number of paupers will be increased. This rent is their main support. Without it they cannot get through the year. Take it from them and they will be ever on the verge of want. This is undoubtedly the cause of the misery of the people of India. The two plans, of private landlords and of the government as a landlord, have been tried; and the result of this experiment demonstrates that a government rent-tax is the parent of poverty. To show this we make two quotations, from Mr. Henry George and from the Duke of Argyll, who was formerly the Governor-General of India:

"In large parts of India, the English, in their desire to create a class of landed proprietors, turned over the soil in absolute possession to hereditary tax-gatherers, who rack-rent the cultivators most mercilessly. In other parts where the rent is still taken by the State in the shape of a land tax, assessments are so high and taxes are collected so relentlessly as to drive the ryots, who get but the most scanty living in good seasons into the claws of money lenders, who are, if possible, more rapacious than the zemindars."—Progress and Poverty, book II, chapter 2.

"India is a country in which theoretically, at least, the State is the only and universal landlord, and over the larger part of it the State does actually take to itself a share of the gross produce which fairly represents ordinary rent. Yet this is the very country in which the poverty of the masses is so abject that millions live only from hand to mouth, and where there is any—even a partial—failure in the crops, thousands and hundreds of thousands are in danger of actual starvation. * * * * Moreover, I could not fail to observe when I was connected with the government of India that the portion of the country which has most grown in wealth is precisely that part of it in which the government has parted with its power of absorbing rent by having agreed to a permanent settlement." The Prophet of San Francisco, pp. 37-8.

The misery of India is caused largely by a rent tax. It is far better when rent is to be paid that it should be paid to the most merciless private landlord than to the most just government. For the private individual has not the powers of the State. When the crops fail he must relinquish or lose a part at least of his rent, and the cultivator lives. But the collection of taxes is and must be relentless.

The statesman on this account tries to make taxation as light as possible. The theorizer would impose a tax that will crush any people into poverty. The people need the rent. To take it from them is to increase poverty indefinitely. Such taxation must destroy all prosperity.

Communism is a Robin Hood, who, for the sake of charity, steals the purses of the nobles and merchants to give them to the widows and orphans. The new political economy, which would destroy the value of land, so that the poor may have the use of it, is a benevolent incendiary who starts a fire that the poor may get the goods that will be thrown out from the burning buildings. The rogues will carry off the goods and the poor will find it harder to live because the stores and factories have been destroyed. Communism is a thief that breaks open a butcher shop to distribute the meat among the hungry. Mr. George would, in his benevolence, set fire to the big barn in the hope that the poor may get some roast beef, never reflecting that the beef will be burnt to a cinder and that the work horses, tools and food of the farm will be burnt, and the farm hands will suffer. Communism is a pious pirate who seizes the ship to give its cargo to the sick and helpless. The new theory is a warm-hearted wrecker, who would bring the ship on the rocks in the belief that the poor would pick up the wreckage. But the cargo will be water-soaked before it reaches the beach of the new paradise, and poverty will be more helpless and hopeless because the ship of state has been wrecked and the fertility of nature has been wasted.

CHAPTER V.

GROUNDS OF OWNERSHIP.

The Strongest Title is Creation—But Man can not have this Title—The Next Strongest is Gift—Illustrations from Childhood—Dicovery—Copyrights and Patent Rights—Occupancy—Purchase—The Landowners Title founded on the Gift of God—On Labor—On Discovery—On Occupancy and Possession—The Assertions of "Progress and Poverty"—They Refute Themselves—They do not go to the Foundations—They are Inconsistent with the Moral Judgment of the Race—Which is the Law of the Creator—Political Economy must hereafter acknowledge the Creator—Property in Land, like Marriage, has sometimes been a Curse—The "Unearned Increment of Land Values"—The Argument Applies to Wages—And to Interest--Justice is the only Safety for all.

The first and strongest title to property is creation. The maker has a right to the thing made. The right of the maker to the product of his work is full, complete and perfect. No one can question it. He has the right against all the world to do as he pleases with it. For this reason God's title to land is indisputable. By creation, the creature, land, belongs to the Creator.

It is very plain that man can not base his

rights of property on his own creation of the things owned. No such full title inheres in man. He does not create. He needs pre-existent materials to work with. He is altogether helpless without land. Without land he can neither work nor exist. He is a manufacturer, but not a creator. The title to property that comes from creation is not his. The laborer who works up the goods of another cannot claim that the article manufactured belongs solely to himself. We are working up the materials of God. We are hands in his factory, shaping anew the raw material that we have taken from land, God's store-house; and we can not claim the exclusive ownership of the manufactured product.

For another reason man can not found his ownership on making. He is not an independent maker. He does not support himself. He is altogether a dependent being. He is by nature a creature and not a creator. Every breath, every pulse, is sustained by God. Only as God preserves his faculties has he any power to labor. Such a laborer can not claim the product of his labor. The labor itself is due to the preserving care of God. Only the independent, self-supporting laborer can claim all the fruits of his labor. Man is not such a laborer.

From labor no perfect title to property can come to man. He cannot make land, and therefore he can create nothing. He is not a self-supporting being, but wholly dependent upon God.

The second ground of ownership is gift. What is given to me, by one having the right to give, is mine. What is bestowed on me by the owner, belongs to me. This is the child's first idea of property. The clothes and the toys given him are his. If given to him absolutely they are his absolutely, if given to him for a purpose they are his for that purpose. Although the clothes belong to him he does not feel that he has a right to cut them to pieces; for they were given to him to wear and not to destroy. The child soon learns the difference between estates. The calf is his to pet but not to sell. The toy is his to play with but not to destroy. The stick is his to whittle. The estate of the recipient depends upon the wishes of the donor, expressed or implied. Estates vary. Some property is given for a short time and some for a longer time; some for one purpose and some for another; some absolutely and some conditionally. The donor may and generally does prescribe the purposes for which the gift is to be used. Only as the property is used in accordance with the donor's prescriptions is the ownership complete and perfect. When the conditions of the gift are violated the right to the gift ends. When the toy is abused, the clothes wantonly destroyed, the pet neglected, the parent righteously takes it from the child. The child feels that he has forfeited his right by failing to use it aright. The legal documents concerning the different kinds of estates aré founded on the primary judgments of mankind.

The relation between God and man is that of giving and receiving. God is the great Giver and man the constant recipient. God's government is providence, for he is always the Provider. Life is his gift. Labor, the power of thought, strength of body, education, time, health, are from him. Land also is his gift to man. Our little book will discuss this fundamental truth, and teach the conditions on which land is given, and the purposes for which it is bestowed.

Discovery is another foundation of ownership. The child quickly sees this truth. What in his wanderings he discovers, a queer pebble, a marble or a penny, he claims. It belongs to him by the right of discovery. But he does not consider that finding gives him as full a title as making or a gift does. The toy windmill that he has made from the stick, the paper and the pin given to him for that purpose, is his absolutely. No one can take it from him without injustice. What is given to him is his, so long as he uses it in accordance with the wishes of the donor. No one else has any right to it. But discovery does not create any such perfect title. The owner may at any time appear and take the thing discovered from him. He may regret the loss, but he feels no indignation. His right to what he has found is good against all others, but imperfect against the one who has a title by labor or by gift.

Copyrights and patent rights are founded on the right of discovery, except perhaps the right to works of fiction and to those whose great value is their style. The poet is a maker. The novelist makes his story. But in more serious works, in books of travel, history, science, philosophy, divinity, law and medicine, the author is rather a discoverer, who exhibits to the world the fruits of his researches. And the inventor has found out some combination of natural forces that will produce a desired result. As the right of discovery is incomplete, not a full and perfect right, the government acts justly in limiting, for the sake of the common benefit, patent rights and copyrights. As it is impossible to distinguish accurately works of learning from works of the imagination, the copyright of all books is limited by law.

By the law of nations, discovery gives to the discoverers a right to uninhabited and uncivilized land which they discover. "On the "discovery of this continent by the nations of "Europe the discovery was considered to have "given to the government by whose subjects "or authority it was made, a title to the coun-"try and the sole right of acquiring the soil "from the natives as against all European "powers." (Kent's Commentaries III, 379). Chancellor Kent shows at length that the rights of the aboriginal Indians were not disregarded, but the land was generally bought of them. The right of discovery is analogous to the right of invention. The Cabots added the territories of the United States to the domains of industry. Watts, by the steam engine, likewise increased the power of labor. It might be a question whether industry had been more aided by discovery or by invention. But the rights of the inventor and of the discoverer are analogous. In both the results are precarious, uncertain and disproportionate to the labor expended. The inventor may spend years without making any useful improvement as the mariner made long voyages without making any important discoveries. The invention or the discovery may be a happy accident. The voyages of the Cabots only cost a few thousands of pounds, and the experiments of Edison only a few thousand dollars. The cost, when success follows, can not be compared with the results. The personal rewards of both inventors and discoverers are uncertain.

A fourth right of property is founded on occupancy. When the chairs of a house are common property, the child feels that he has a right to the chair in which he is sitting. If he leaves it some one else may take it. But as long as he continues to use it, no other child has the right to disturb him. If the seats of a park, a steamer or a church have been provided for those visiting these places, each visitor has a right to the seat he is occupying. Any one dispossessing him is a transgressor. So long as he occupies it in accordance with the rules of the place his title is good. But if he abandons it his right ceases, and any one can occupy the seat without doing him any wrong. His claim by occupancy prevails over any one who has no other claim. But it is plain that occupancy, like discovery, does not give a perfect title to property. It must yield to the title that comes of labor and to the title that comes of gift. If the seats have been reserved by those having the authority to dispose of them, the occupants must move. Occupancy only creates a title to what is common property—a title which lasts only so long as the occupancy continues.

To one or more of these reasons must all title to property be referred. Ownership may rest on one or it may rest on several or on all of these grounds, but unless it rests on at least one of them it can not be defended.

The reader may wonder that we have said nothing of purchase as a foundation of ownership. By purchase most property rights in the world begin. Yet it has no place in our analysis. For bargain and sale is merely the transferring of rights. The buyer gives his rights to one thing in exchange for the seller's rights to another thing. I give my money for meat, that is my right to the coin for the butcher's right to the beef. Purchase creates no property rights. It merely exchanges one for another.

Property in land is based upon all four of these grounds of ownership. The land owner's title is grounded on the right of labor, on gift, on discovery and on occupancy.

Our first chapter asserted the truth, that land belongs to the Creator because he made it by his own independent powers, out of nothing. But he did not make it for himself. He made it to be inhabited. "The earth hath he given to the children of men." Government is his agent. The powers that be are ordained of God. Through civil government God's right to land is transferred to men. A full discussion of this point will be found in subsequent chapters. The theory of our law agrees with that of "The Bible and Land." Blackstone states the English law as follows:

"It became a fundamental and necessary principle (though in reality a mere fiction) of our English tenures that the King is the universal lord and original proprietor of all the lands in his kingdom; and that no man doth or can possess any part of it but what has mediately or immediately been derived as a gift from him to be held on feudal tenure."—Commentaries, II, 51.

"All the land in the kingdom is supposed to be holden, mediately or immediately, of the King, who is styled the lord paramount or above all."—Commentaries, II, 59.

The theory of American law is the same.

"The people in their right of sovereignty are deemed to possess the original and ultimate property in and to all lands within the jurisdiction of the State."—Constitution of New York, 1846.

"It is a settled and valid doctrine with us that all valid title to land within the United States is derived from the grant of our own local government or from that of the United States or from the crown or royal chartered governments established here prior to the Revolution. * * * It was held to be a settled doctrine that the courts could not take notice of any title to land not derived from our own State or colonial government, and duly verified by patent. This was also a fundamental principle in the colonial jurisprudence. All titles to land passed to individuals from the crown, though the colonial corporations and the colonial or proprietary authorities."—Kent's Commentaries, III, 378.

If therefore civil government is the ordinance of God, the land owner, holding his land from the State, holds it by the gift of the Creator.

Property in land is also founded on labor. Its value and utility have been largely produced by labor. The forests have been felled, the fields fenced, cleared of stumps and rocks, drained, ploughed and enriched by the land owner, or by those whose rights have been inherited or purchased. More labor must be expended to produce a given value in agricultural land than in any form of manufacture. If an account had been kept, and the land charged with the labor expended upon it and credited with the crops produced, it would be found that more labor had been spent in producing a hundred dollars worth of farming land than would be necessary to produce a hundred dollars worth of hats or shoes or other goods. It is notorious that agricultural wages are low and farmers' profits small. The fields have been enriched by the farmer's feet and watered by his sweat. If ordinary farming lands were sold it would not pay fair wages for the labor expended upon it during the several generations it has been tilled, that has not been paid for by crops. A large part—much the larger part—of the value of agricultural lands is the result of labor.

We admit that all land value is not caused by labor. The same is true of wealth, of all manufactures. A part of the value of the hat consists in the wool—the raw material out of which the hat is made. But both in the value of land and of manufactures labor has been so intermingled with the unartificial materials furnished by nature that it is practically impossible to separate them, and to say what part of the value is due to labor and what to nature. If the farmer has no title to his fields because nature has supplied the wilderness out of which the fields are made, the furniture maker has no title to his wares because nature supplied the lumber from which they were made. The original value cannot be separated from the value created by labor—both belong to the producer, whether the product is a hat or a farm.

This title, the right of property that comes from producing, is not, we may admit, as strong as that which comes from gift. The one who mixes his labor with the goods of another can not justly claim the whole value of the thing made from those goods. But the land-owner's title in this respect is as strong as that of the manufacturer.

The land-owner has also by purchase or inheritance all right of property that springs from discovery or occupancy. Blackstone bases all right of ownership in land on occupancy; but this is inconsistent with the "fundamental maxim and necessary principles of our English tenures," as stated by him. But whatever right comes from discovery and long and undisturbed possession and occupancy, belongs to the land-owner.

The American land-owner possesses by purchase, or inheritance, all the rights that the Indian had, whether by gift of God, discovery or possession; all the right that the Crown, the colonial governments, the federal or State governments had, whether by gift of the Creator, by discorery or by occupancy. All the grounds that create property rights support his claim to the exclusive ownership of his land. The terms, on which God gives land to man, will be enquired into hereafter. But if there is such a thing as property the land-owner has it, by grant of God, by labor, by discovery and by occupancy and possession. Of all property landed property is the oldest. The title of the American land-owner is older than the State and national governments, older than the colonial governments, older than history itself.

Mr. Henry George denies that land can be rightfully property. His argument is stated in the following extracts from "Progress and Poverty."

"Nature acknowledges no ownership or control in man save as the result of exertion." "There can be to the ownership of anything no rightful title which is not derived from the title of the producer, and does not rest upon the natural right of the man himself." "The laws of nature are the decrees of the Creator. There is written in them no natural right save that of labor; and in them is written broadly and clearly the equal right of all men to the use and enjoyment of nature." "The right of ownership that springs from labor excludes the possibility of any other right of ownership." "When non-producers can claim as rent a portion of the wealth created by producers, the rights of the producers to the fruits of their labor is to that extent denied." "Whatever may be said for the institution of private property in land it is therefore plain that it cannot be defended on the score of justice." "The equal rights of all men to the use of the land is as clear as their equal right to breathe the air—is is a right proclaimed by the fact of their existence." Progress and Poverty, book VII. ch. 1.

Mr. George dare not carry his principle to its legitimate conclusion. He states it himself: "The equal rights of all men to the use "of land is as clear as their equal right to "breathe the air." Wherever the man is he breathes. He has a right to breathe. Whoever tries to stop his breathing is a garrotter, a murderer, to be resisted. Whatever interferese with his breathing he instinctively and righteously (unless his life is forfeited) removes at once by force. Apply the same principle to land. Let every one try to appropriate land as he appropriates air. The result will be immediate and universal anarchy, savagery, desolation. Our wealth would be annihilated, our civilization destroyed and our population decimated, within a year. Manifestly there is a difference between land and air. The one is limited in amount, has value, and is property. The other is unlimited in amount, has no value, and is not property.

As Mr. George dare not carry his principles

to their necessary conclusion he proposes an expedient which is inconsistent with the principles quoted above. This expedient we examined in the last chapter. We have seen that it would necessarily produce despotism, encourage the wasting of nature and lead to universal poverty. By the fruit we may judge of the tree. Its necessary results condemu thea ssertion that land ought not to be property.

We will not, however, judge by the fruit alone. We will analyze the root. Whence comes "the natural right of a man to himself?" Is it the result of labor? Did he make himself? Did he create the power to think or the power to work? Plainly it is the gift of God. He has a right to himself because God gave him to himself, and only so far and for such purposes as God gave him to himself. His labor belongs partly to his wife and his children and partly to society, and partly to God. Labor is the gift of God; and land is also the gift of the Creator. Both rights, the right to labor and the right to land, spring from God's gift. Land ownership is the result of creation. It is founded on the same basis as the natural right to labor.

The laws of society are, equally with the laws of nature, the decrees of the Creator. And in these laws of society, the private ownership of land is fundamental. Everywhere and always in human society, land has been property. As far back as we can go, all desirable land has had an owner. There may have been some undiscovered island, or barren snow field or sahara or jungle or swamp that has no owner, but it was because no one could use it. Wherever land has had utility it has been property. Many tribes indeed have held and used their land in common. But they have not admitted the right of any others in them. They have resented and resisted the intrusion of other tribes into their territories. The common use of land is the best way for hunters, and shepherds to enjoy their land. It was impossible for the hunters to fence their game. A wide range was better for the sheep or cattle. .When there was only a rude tillage it was unwise to fence the fields which were only to be ploughed for one or two seasons. They had their territories in common for the same reasons that the stockholders hold their railroad in common, it was the wisest way to use their property. The common possession of the tribe implied the right of its members.

The tribe was a joint stock company to defend and enjoy its lands. Everywhere as the game disappeared, as agriculture supplanted the feeding of sheep, as commerce, diversified industry and civilization advanced, the tribal use of land gave place to the individual use of land. But land was as much property before the change as it was after it: for tribal and private ownership of land are only different forms of property in land.

Everywhere and always land has been property. This law of society is the decree of the Creator. The reason of this law we have seen. Land value and the ownership of land are needed to protect land from being abused and wasted.

The question of the rightfulness of private property in land is an ethical question. All races, all men, have thought more or less about it, and all, except Mr. George and his followers, have decided that land should be property. No philosopher has ever changed the ethical judgment of the race. Galileo changed the world's opinion in regard to astronomy, Hunter in regard to physiology, and Priestly in regard to air. These are subjects on which all do not care to think; but ethics interest all. All have not the data of science; but all possess the data of ethics. No merely human teacher has ever reversed the moral judgments of the race, and the race has decided that land ownership is righteous.

The great benefit of Mr. George's work is that it compels political economy to acknowledge the truths of natural religion. There are only two alternatives: Either property, of all kinds, is the gift of God or it is the product of labor. If it is the result of labor, land is not property; for it existed before work began and would continue to exist should work cease. If property is the gift of God, all property, but especially land, must be accepted on the terms which the Creator attaches to his gifts. Either the private ownership of land is unrighteous, or it must be used as God prescribes.

Another argument against the private ownership of land that runs all through "Progress and Poverty," (though nowhere expressly stated) is that it has been the means of oppression and extortion. The fact is acknowledged. By it landlords have lived dissolutely while tenants starved. The same is true of other institutions of God. The family has enabled husbands to abuse their wives and train their children in crime. It would be hard to defend the divorce laws of New England against the criticisms of a Mormon elder. It would be difficult to defend Nero against the ten commandments or the Czar against the golden rule. Nevertheless the family, monogamy and civil government have done more good than harm. The benefits that have come from the private ownership of land can neither be counted nor weighed.

Another argument against the rightfulness of property in land is that land value is the creation of society and not of the land-owner, and that therefore it belongs to society and not to the land-owners. In a desert isle, land is worth nothing. When it is densely settled land is valuable. The land value is caused by population, and therefore it should righteously belong to the people, and not to the land-owner. Much is said about "the unearned increment of land values." Manhattan Island, for example, at one time was worth only twenty-five dollars. Now it is worth hundreds of millions. The increase in value has been caused by the erection of New York city on the island. As the city has created the land value it belongs (it is said) to the city and not to the land-owners.

If the reasoning is good it should apply to others than land-owners. Increase of population increases other values as well as land values. It increases the value of labor. Poor Robinson Crusoe worked for months to build a canoe. The result of his long labor was a boat that would have been worth nothing in a civilized community, except as a curiosity or as firewood. His bag of gold, his wealth, was worth nothing to him. In his desert island labor and wealth (the product of labor) were as valueless as the land. As society increased, all would acquire value. When Manhattan Island was worth twenty-five dollars, the savages made a rude and precarious living. Their wigwams were worse shelters than the darkest room in a tenement house. Their clothing was rude. Their food was often scanty. The total result of a year's exertion was worth probably less than fifty dollars. A dollar a week in New York city would purchase better shelter, clothing and food. With less fatigue, exposure and skill, the male workers of New York city earn from three hundred dollars a year upward. This is not the result of greater skill or industry. The Indian was master of a dozen trades, the citizen knows only a part of one. The Indian followed his game through rain and snow; the citizen exposes himself but little. This increase of wages has come from population and civilization. It is caused by society. It is an "unearned increment" of labor. If the unearned increment of land belongs to society, so does the unearned increment of labor. Both must be judged by the same principle.

Wealth also increases in value without labor. Trees grow, cattle multiply, grain ripens, wine mellows. These increases in value are not the result of labor. They come in part from civil order. Without it they could not occur. They are the work of society, and if the unearned increment of land belongs to society, these also belong to the public.

The increase or profits justly belong to the owner. Land value belongs to the land owner, wages to the laborer and interest to the capitalist. If land increases in value the landowner is benefitted. If wages rise, the laborer righteously claims the advantage. If the rate of interest rises the capitalist justly claims the increase. Good government, civil order, the progress of civilization—in a word, society—do raise the value of land, the rewards of labor and the security and productiveness of capital. Social order probably benefits the laborer and capitalist more than it does the land-owner. But this gives to the State no right to claim either wages or interest on land value. For in protecting life, wealth and land, government (society) has merely done its duty. If the present generation seizes the land by confiscating rent, the next generation may enslave labor or steal capital. It has as much right to these as it has to land value. It has enabled the laborer to work in peace, or to secure for his toil a much greater reward than he could in a savage state. It has protected the capitalist and has defended him in loaning his money and in collecting interest. Justice is the security of all. Injustice towards one class opens the way to tyranny towards all classes.

CHAPTER VI.

THE TERMS OF THE ORIGINAL GRANT.

Every Good Deed to Land must begin with "I Give"—The Original Grant is Recorded in Genesis—Blackstone's Exposition of it—His Error—Its Terms—Must be Complied with—Otherwise Land is Forfeited—It was Forfeited by the Antediluvians—The Second Grant. (NOTE on the Malthusian Theory—Is False—Removes all Feeling of Responsibility for Poverty—And Blasphemes God.)

The ownership of land must rest on the grant of the Creator. Every real deed to land must begin "I give and grant." Only on creation can we found a full, perfect and complete title to land. It can not be built on human labor; for land is not the result of our labor. Discovery and occupation will give a possessory title, good perhaps against other claimants, but not such a title as we need to resist the assertions of "Progress and Poverty," that landed property is unjust. But a title from God needs no defense. Such is the title we believe that the land-owner has. God made the land. He did not make it for himself but for man. The universal laws of society are that land is property and rightfully belongs to the land-owner; and that land should have value for its protection, which will be low when population is scant and lands need little protection, and high when population is dense and lands need more protection. The laws of society, the true principles of political economy, are the decrees of God. Land titles come from God.

Upon what terms does God give land to man? What are the conditions of the grant? For what purposes may man use land? These are vital questions. To answer them we go to the Bible, not because it contains the history of redemption, but because it gives us an infallible account of the principles of truth and justice which we need now and here in our own country. Concerning faith and repentance we are not now enquiring. What are the principles of natural religion that should govern our land legislation? What are the conditions of God's grants? What kind of an estate in land do we possess? As an infallible revelation from God the Bible will answer these questions correctly.

The land is God's because he made it. We need it and he gives it to us; but upon what conditions? To answer this question we go where no political economist, so far as we know, has ever gone, to the account of the creation in the first chapter of Genesis. No sect nor party has doubted that our first parents were to some extent the natural representatives of their descendants, and that what was given to them in this chapter was in them given to their descendants. There have been debates as to the precise nature of the federal headship of Adam, but none have ever questioned the fact, that the race are the heirs of Adam and Eve. In this chapter we find these words spoken to Adam soon after the creation:

"And God blessed them, and God said unto them: Be fruitful and multiply and replenish the earth and subdue it; and have dominion over the fish of the sea and over the fowl of the air, and over every living thing that moveth upon the face of the earth."—Genesis 1:28.

This command was given in Adam to his descendants. And the grant contained in it, extended to them. Sir William Blackstone expounds this passage as follows:

"In the beginning of the world we are told by Holy Writ, the all bountiful Creator gave to man 'dominion over all the earth, and over the fish of the sea and over the fowls of the air, and over every living thing that moveth upon the earth.' This is the only true and solid foundation for man's dominion over external things, whatever airy, metaphysical notions may have been started by fanciful writers upon the subject. The earth, therefore, and all things therein are the general property of all mankind, exclusive of other beings, from the immediate gift of the Creator. And while the earth continued bare of inhabitants, it is reasonable to suppose, that all was in common among them, and that every one took from the public stock to his own use such things as his immediate necessities required. These general notions of property were then sufficient to answer all the purposes of human life; and might perhaps still have answered them, had it been possible for man to have remained in a state of primeval simplicity." Commentaries, II, 2 and 3.

"The only true and solid foundation of man's dominion over external things" is God's gift. All other foundations are "airy, metaphysical notions, started by fanciful writers." Why does not Blackstone base his theories of "the rights of things" on this "only true and solid foundation?" Why does he forsake it to build on the airy, metaphysical notion of occupancy confirmed by usage?

The answer is plain. The land laws of England could not rest on it. The land laws of the world do not and can not rest upon God's deed to man.

Blackstone interprets this text as bestowing an undivided estate to be divided afterwards by men as their opinions might dictate. He states that by this grant the earth became the general property of all mankind, the common possession of all. If he had been as careless in interpreting human laws as he is in interpreting the divine law, which he does not even quote accurately, he would have had little reputation as a lawyer. For there is nothing in the passage about general property. It is placed there by Blackstone. The text defines the purposes for which land is to be used. But it does not prescribe the modes by which it is to be applied to these purposes. It says nothing about general or separate property.* The text might allow a general property if the purposes of the grant could be thus better fulfilled; but it does not prescribe it. Even in that state of "primeval simplicity," separate possessions would better fulfill the purposes of the grant.

* In passing, we remark that the Bible nowhere approves the "nationalization" of land. The nationalization of the land of Egypt in the time of Joseph is only an apparent exception.

Eve would want an exclusive interest, and not a general property, in her flower beds in Eden. Cain needed the exclusive possession of his fields, and Abel the exclusive possession of a spot on which to build his sheep-fold. A general property would not answer their purposes. The deed must be carefully construed. Nothing can be imported into it. And Blackstone's idea of a general property is not in it. Such an idea is contrary to the other land grants recorded in the Bible. Canaan was given first to the Amorite and next to Israel in individual ownership. Seir was given to Esau, Moab and the surrounding country to the children of Lot. "The earth hath he given," not to the race, and not to the rulers, but "to the children of men."

The grant recorded in the account of the creation must be strictly construed. The land by it is given to the children of Adam only for certain purposes. If the conditions are not complied with, the grant fails; and the land reverts to God. If men do not use it for these purposes they have not, any longer, any just title to it. The deed has been recorded, and it must be complied with.

It is evident also that those who inherit

from our first parents can have no greater estate in the land than they had. If they took it on conditions, the conditions bind their heirs. The original grant governs subsequent conveyances. We can have no greater right, as we have other right, to land than that given in the original deed.

The conditions of the grant are three. It is reasonable to suppose that they have been arranged in the order of their importance. The first condition is that the land is to be used to sustain population, in such circumstances as are conducive to health and holiness, to morality and intelligence. The command, "Be fruithful and multiply and replenish the earth" * does not refer merely to numbers; for "the Lord sought a holy seed." The land is to be used to support population in a state that will be favorable to virtue. The second condition is that man is to subdue the land, by draining swamps, thinning forests, opening mines, building roads, deepening harbors, tunneling mountains, bridging rivers, laying out parks and in all other ways that will add to the health, holiness, comfort and pleasure of mankind. The third condition is that man

* The Malthusian theory will be treated separately.

is to master and rule the brutes, and to be to them in some sort a representative of God. Only so far as man seeks to comply with these conditions has he any righteous claim to land.

Let us re-state the argument. What right have I to my home? The enquiry is not about the legal title. On what is the legal right based? Why can I claim an exclusive property in my own land? I did not make the land, and so I cannot claim it as the result of my labor. Occupancy, even prior occupancy, (though I have that claim) can not create a perfect title. The tacit consent of mankind, or the social compact, will not create such a title; for plainly, men can not by consent give what they did not before possess. No other ground is left but the gift of God. The land is mine because God has given it to me, through the State, his minister for this purpose, by means of discovery, occupancy, established law and custom; through inheritance, bequest or purchase. As my ownership is derived from God it is indisputable. But, as God granted it for certain purposes, I can rightfully enjoy it only so long as I use it for those purposes. If I do not comply with the conditions of the grant, I am a trespasser. Thus the true doctrine about land binds the land-owner very closely to God.

It may be said that there is a long chain between the Creator and the land-owner—a great distance between the creation and owning land in the United States. It is true. God works indeed by many agencies. No deist will deny that his life is God's gift. Consider the vast number of agencies he employs to create and continue that life—agencies of every kind; bodily, political, commercial, agricultural, reaching back to Adam's day. The instruments he uses to bestow land are no more numerous than those used to maintain life.

The early history of the world confirms this account of landed property. For the antediluvians did not use land to feed virtue. "The wickedness of man was great in the earth" (or "on the land"). The Lord therefore destroyed them "from the face of the ground." By wickedness, by failing to comply with the conditions of the grant, the race, with the exception of one family, had forfeited the grant. Man was therefore removed from the earth, except Noah's family. By man's sin, the land had reverted to the Creator. He can give it to whom he pleases and on what conditions he pleases.

The grant to Noah differs in two respects from that to Adam. It is, as regards the whole race, irrevocable. Individuals may be destroyed; but the race shall not be, while the earth remaineth. It also includes animal food which was not in the grant to Adam. But the main condition of the two grants is the same. The land is given to Noah, and in Noah to his heirs, to support population.

"And God blessed Noah and his sons and said unto them be fruitful and multiply and replenish the earth. And the fear of you and the dread of you shall be upon every beast of the earth and upon every fowl of the air; with all wherewith the ground teemeth, and all the fishes of the sea, into your hand are they delivered."—Genesis 9, 1-2.

The manner in which land is to be used is not here prescribed. The purpose for which it is to be used is very plainly stated. It is to support population. All right to land since the flood flows from this grant to Noah. As his heirs we have no greater estate in land than he had. We can only use it for the purpose for which it was given to Noah. As the grant to him was conditional, our ownership of land is not absolute. We must use it to supply human wants.

NOTE ON THE MALTHUSIAN THEORY.

We do not deem it necessary to refute the Malthusian theory. Our whole book is an answer to it. But a theory that has had and still has such a wide influence can not be ignored.

The theory ascribes human misery to the growth of population. It asserts, as a general law, that population tends to outrun production. As a general law this is simply and only a falsehood. In peculiar cases it may be true. When Robinson Crusoe dwelt alone on his desert island, population was in excess of production when he fell sick. In times of war or famine or pestilence, there may not have been enough to supply the wants of the community. In an island cut off from the rest of the world, and unable to exchange its labor for that of others, production may be insufficient for human wants. But as a general law it is false. There is not now and there never has been any country that did not or could not produce enough to supply all of its inhabitants with the necessities and many of the comforts of life. There has been pauperism and misery in the world, but to ascribe them to a law of nature is a slander upon God. Instead of population outrunning production, production increases faster than population. Labor becomes more effective as the people increase. Two men can do more than twice as much as one man. With Friday's help Crusoe could do ten times as much as he could by himself. Twenty laborers can do more than ten times as much as two. With every increase in population there is an increase in the effectiveness of labor, even when there is no invention. And the poorest nation (unless it was some degraded and small band of savages) has had wealth to supply all of the wants of its members.

The misery in the world is not because enough is not produced to supply the wants of all, but it is because what is produced is unequally distributed. If land is used for the support of pride, profusion and profligacy, instead of being used for the support of population, if labor is uselessly employed, instead of being used for production, there may be an insufficiency of things needed by man; but there has never been such a case; and if it should arise it ought to be ascribed to the wickedness of man in misusing land and labor, rather than to any lack of capacity in them.

The reason why the theory has prevailed so widely is that it saves man the trouble of enquiring into the causes of poverty, and enables the rich to enjoy their prosperity with untroubled consciences. By ascribing pauperism to natural law, it removes all feeling of responsibility for it. It really throws the blame of pauperism on the Creator who commands the race to multiply. It is therefore not only false; not only opposed to the highest, purest and noblest instincts of humanity, but it is also blasphemous, as it charges God with the poverty and pauperism caused by human greed.

CHAPTER VII.

BIBLICAL LAND GRANTS.

The Use of the Biblical Histories—The History of Adam—The True Owner of Canaan—He Gives Land to Men—But not to Nations or to Rulers—The Apparent Exception in Egypt Examined—How he Gives Land—The Title of the Amorites—Of Edom—Of Moab—The Grants may be Forfeited—As in Canaan—In Seir—And in Moab—Our Own Inheritance.

The Bible histories are useful as samples of history. Their great advantage is that in them we learn how God regards human annals. Our historians can only show us the human side of the tapestry which is woven by the co-operation of God and man. The Bible shows us specimens of the other side. From these samples we learn that God is interested in all human events, and that the events which we think of as merely human, are also divine. From the Bible histories we learn that God gives land to men, and that he gives it to them conditionally.

Abram, (a native of Mesopotamia) moved with Terah his father to Haran where his father died. God commanded Abram, (how we know not) to go "unto a land which I will show thee." As soon as he entered Canaan, "the Lord appeared unto Abram and said unto him. Unto thy seed will I give this land." After a time Abram and Lot separated on a mountain near Bethel, from which there was a wide prospect; for Lot (we read) "Lifted up his eyes and beheld all the plain of Jordan." After the separation, God said to Abram, "Lift up now thy eyes, and look from the place where thou art, northward and southward, and eastward and westward; for all the land which thou seest to thee will I give it and to thy seed forever. * * * Arise walk through the land, in the length of it and in the breadth of it, for I will give it unto thee."

After the rescue of Lot by Abram, God more formally entered into a covenant with him, in the mode then in use for the ratification of treaties. It was revealed to Abram that his descendants should be "a stranger in a land that is not theirs and shall serve them, and they shall afflict them four hundred years." "But in the fourth generation they shall come hither again; for the iniquity of the Amorites is not yet full." The last clause is added as the reason why, for a time, the descendants of Abram should be excluded from a land that had just been granted to them.

From this narrative, passing over other truths, we can learn some facts about land.

One is that God is the owner of land. It is acknowledged in general terms that the earth is the Lord's; but only a vague indefinite meaning is attached to the phrase. Here it is very definite. It is the land of Canaan in its length and breadth which God claims the right to dispose of: the plains and hills in sight from the mountain near Bethel. There is no difference, in this respect, between Canaan and other countries, between this and other mountain views. God's ownership of land is a fundamental fact of political economy, a primary truth of law and social science.

Another truth is, that God gives land to men. He gave Canaan to Abram. Some of the circumstances of the grant were unusual; and there were good reasons for these departures from the usual methods of providence. In the grant itself there was nothing peculiar. As he gave Canaan to the Israelites, so he gave portions to other nations. In the days of Peleg (Genesis, 10: 25) "was the earth divided."

"The Most High gave to the nations their inheritance, when he separated the children of men, he set the bounds of the people according to the number of the children of Israel." (Deuteronomy 32: 8.) "I have given Mount Seir unto Esau for a possession." (Deuteronomy 2: 4). "I have given Ar unto the children of Lot for a possession." (Deuteronomy 2: 9). "I will not give thee of the land of the children of Ammon; because I have given it to the children of Lot for a possession." (Deuteronomy 2: 19). "The earth hath he given to the children of men." (Psalms 115: 16). "I have made the earth, the man and the beasts that are upon the face of the earth, by my great power and by my outstretched arm; and I give it unto whom it seemeth right unto me." (Jeremiah 27: 5). "And hath made of one blood all nations of men for to dwell on all the face of the earth, and hath determined the times before appointed and the bounds of their habitation." (Acts 17: 26.) We demand that all land theories, political economy and land legislation shall stand upon this truth, that God gives land to men.

The gift of God makes, not nations and not rulers, but individuals, the land-owners. The nationalization of land is not countenanced by the inspired history of God's land grants. It is true that the eastern mode of speaking is used, and Canaan is given to Israel, Seir to Esau, and "the Most High gave to the nations their inheritance;" but no forced meaning is to be placed on such expressions. We have no reason to suppose that the lands of Seir were used exclusively for the public benefit. And although Canaan is again and again declared to be given to Israel, yet this expression is not inconsistent with private property in land. In Palestine, by the special direction of God, land was private property. The land was divided by the command of God, at the door of his tabernacle, by his priest, among the Israelites. Their portions were made inalienable—a perpetual private possession. We say that England belongs to the English, France to the French, Holland to the Dutch. We do not mean by this that the rent of English lands is taken by the English government for public purposes, but that the English soil is owned by Englishmen We do not mean that France and Holland are public property, but that the soil is owned by Frenchmen and Dutchmen. A like interpretation is to be placed upon the texts quoted in the last paragraph. We assert that God's gift creates private property in land as distinguished from a public or national ownership.

The Bible nowhere sanctions the national ownership of land. The only apparent exception is in the case of Egypt when the lands during the famine were bought by Joseph for Pharaoh. The rents of the soil were henceforth appropriated for public purposes and used to build pyramids; very much as Mr. George would confiscate the rent of American land for public purposes, and use it to buy railroads and to support public dance houses and theatres. But the Bible in recording the acts, even of good men, does not thereby sanction them. It may also be said that, so far as we can see, no other course was open to Joseph. The grain needed the protection of value. If he had given it away, it would have been wasted. Only by putting a high price on it could Joseph make it last through the seven years of famine. It may also be remarked that the narrative is very brief. It is evident that even before the famine Pharaoh possessed the power of levying heavy taxes. (See Genesis 41: 48, 49.) A great tax, perhaps a half or a third of the crop, would have been necessary to provide in seven years the means to support the people for seven years. The change may have been merely a change from an indefinite to a fixed and definite power of taxation. We can not use this obscure case to attack the truth that the Biblical land grants make land private property.

The method in which Canaan was granted to Abram differed in two respects from the methods in which other lands were granted to other nations. There were revelations and miracles. The reason for these differences is plain. Abram was not only an eastern sheik, but also the founder of the Church and the father of the faithful. As Abram stood in a different relation to God than other sheiks, it was proper that different modes should be used in giving him land. We are not to exaggerate these differences; but we are to remember that the Jews were a nation like other nations; and Canaan was like other countries, subject to the same laws of political economy, and of national growth and decay.

God had previously given Canaan to the Amorites. They had no visions or revelations from God, but the land was theirs. The visions are not seals essential to the validity of divine deeds to land, but merely a phraseology, so to speak, that was suitable only in the case of Israel. Although the Amorites had no visions, their land title was perfect. God himself respected it. He wished to give Canaan to Abram; but he will not suffer Israel to possess it until the iniquity of the Amorites is full, and they have forfeited their title. Although Canaan had been promised to Israel they must abide in a strange land until the prior title has been forfeited. The land has been promised to Abram and his seed forever; but when he wished a burial place he bought it. The exclusive ownership of the Amorites was recognized in every way. God acknowledges it: Abram acts on it; and his seed suffer by it.

It was the same in other lands. "I have given Mount Seir unto Esau for a possession." (See Deuteronomy, ch. 2, v. 4, 5, 12, 22.) Edom was not the people of God; and indeed, they could not enter the congregation of the Lord till the third generation. Their title deeds to Mount Seir were written in blood; for they were not the original inhabitants of their country, but they had exterminated their predecessors. Israel was a homeless race, weary with long wanderings. They had the power to seize the country for Esau feared them. "Meddle not with them; for I will not give you of their land; no, not so much as a hand's breadth, because I have given Mount Seir unto Esau for a possession." Here we have another instance of the ownership of land respected by God himself.

Moab was the richest land near Canaan. It also lay in the pathway of the landless nation. But Israel was warned not to vex Moab "for I will not give thee of his land for a possession; because I have given Ar unto the children of Lot for a possession." The Moabites had no special claim upon God; they could not enter into his congregation till the tenth generation; and they were not the original inhabitants of their land. Yet God protected their title against Israel. If Israel had seized Moab, it would have been in rebellion against God. If God makes land private property, whoever attacks the private ownership of land, fights against God.

From those histories another fact is manifest. Land may be forfeited. The land grants of God are rather leases than deeds in fee simple. Conditions are attached to them.

When the conditions are not complied with the land reverts to God who gives it to others, or leaves it vacant, as seems best to him. The Amorites' title to Canaan was full and perfect. Yet afterwards it reverted to God who gave it to Israel. It was given to the Amorites to support virtue, but they used it to feed vice. When, after a trial of four hundred years, it was plain that the Amorites would not use it to support population in circumstances favorable to piety, the land reverted to God. The cup of their iniquity filled up gradually. Abuse followed abuse, one evil led to another. It was a slow progress. They were probably priding themselves on their superiority over other nations when Israel crossed Jordan dry shod, and the vengeance of God fell on them; and their forfeited lands were given to others.

Esau afterwards forfeited Mount Seir. Their national sin seems to have been hatred and war. Instead of using Mount Seir to support a peaceful population they used it as a fortress. Moab forfeited Ar. Its sin may have been pride. Instead of giving their lands to other nations God has left them desolate, as monuments, on which other ages may read the truth that the land grants of God are conditional, and that land, if misused, reverts to the Creator.

Israel afterwards forfeited Canaan. Its rulers decreed unrighteousness, turned the needy from judgment, and made widows their prey. Its elders ground the faces of the poor. Its rich men joined field to field. The daughters of Zion were extravagant. The whole nation was corrupt. "From the sole of the feet "unto the head there is no soundness in it; but "wounds and bruises and putrefying sores." (Isaiah 1: 6). Therefore the prophet adds: "Your country is desolate; your cities are "burned with fire; your land, strangers devour "it in your presence, and it is desolate, as "overthrown by strangers." (Isaiah 1: 7). Israel lost Canaan; not by external force, but by internal corruption. And so may our people lose their country. Canaan is kept comparatively empty, waiting for Israel to repent.

God has given to our people a vast inheritance. But we are not the absolute owners of it. We can not do as we please with it. Our land must be used to support an industrious and frugal population. If we employ it to sustain extravagance and ostentation, we misuse it, and it is forfeited. May we be found not unworthy of our vast inheritance!

There is a dim resemblance between the history of Canaan and America. The Anakim preceded the dawn of history in Canaan, and the mound builders in America. The Canaanitish tribes lost their lands when the cup of their iniquity was filled up. And the Indian tribes have been banished from their lands. The tribes of Canaan were nearly extinguished, and the Indian tribes are hastening forward on the same road. Israel prospered for a while but fell into sin and lost their country. May we take warning from their fate.

CHAPTER VIII.

THE LAND LAWS OF MOSES.

The Bible Teaches by Illustration—Example—The Mosaic Code a Parable About Land—In Accord with Truth and Justice—Easier Understood than History and Philosophy—Its Seven Fundamental Principles—1. The Land is God's—2. Land Titles are Based on God's Gift—3. He Gives it Conditionally—4. It May be Forfeited—5. It Should be Private Property—6. Laws about Land and about Wealth should Differ—Reasons for it—7. Land Should be Subject to Special Burdens—Advantages of the Land Tax—Easier Collected—The Government gets all that is Collected from the People—Does Not Check Production—Is not Demoralizing—Will Purify Government—Is Just.

The Bible is the briefest and most interesting of all law books. When compared with codes that cover far less ground, its brevity is surprising. Legal books interest only a few, the Bible interests all. The cause of this difference is not very obscure. Human codes of law deal with specific prohibitions. The Bible uses illustrative examples. The human law-giver must state with exact precision, what deeds he will punish, and how he will punish them. The divine Law-giver gives a single example that throws light on all similar cases. If the legislature should try to enjoin on its citizens the duties of humanity, it would enact a dry law book, which the courts would expand into twenty volumes of decisions. The heavenly Law-giver teaches the same duties by the parable of the good Samaritan, a very short and interesting anecdote, which teaches the duty of kindness between all men in all the relations of life.

The land legislation of Moses is a parable about land. The Mosaic code is useful to us as an exhibition of the fundamental principles of justice. As it was designed for a peculiar people, in a peculiar country, in peculiar relations to Jehovah, it is not suited to other nations and other ages. The great mistake of those who have sought political guidance from the Bible, has been that they looked for rules, and not for principles, for specific laws and not for the maxims of righteousness that should underlie all laws. The Jewish code would be a bad code for us. Our system of law is better for our age and country than it would be. And yet in this divinely inspired code we may find those principles of equity on which all land legislation should rest.

As the Mosaic code was made by God, its

fundamental maxims (if we can discover them) must be in accord with justice, righteousness and truth, everywhere and always. The application of these principles does, and must, vary in different countries and at different times. But the principles must be true, because divine, always and everywhere.

We may err in trying to find the fundamental principles of the Mosaic code. We may mistake the accidental for the essential. We may confound what was only suited to Palestine with what is suited to land everywhere. But, to say the least, we are in no more danger of erring here than elsewhere. The great work of the coming generation of America is to discover and to apply to land the great principles of truth and righteousness that should govern all land legislation. To discover these principles, we may go to history and society, or we may go to the Bible. The teachings of history are confusing; the facts of society clash; the maxims of law are unsatisfactory; the teaching of political and social science, is the prattle of children. It is easier to understand Moses than to unravel the facts of society, or to decipher the lessons of history. When the problem is solved it will be found that God and truth, the fundamental principles of the Mosaic code and of good government everywhere, are in full accord. But the easiest way to solve the problem, which must be solved if we are to save America from the fate of Judea, Greece and Rome, is to go to the Mosaic code. Moses speaks more plainly than political economy. God's parable about land is more easily comprehended than man's philosophy.

One fundamental principle of the Mosaic code is, that the land belongs to God. He claims it: "The land is mine." (Leviticus 25:23). It is not necessary to prove this, as none, except atheists, deny it. But legislation and political economy ignore it. The great master of English law (as we have seen) is satisfied with a vague compliment to the "bountiful Creator." The astronomer who should try to explain the facts of the solar system, without making any reference to the attraction of gravitation, would err more and more the longer he speculated. The physiologist who should write about the body and ignore the circulation of the blood, would fall into a great error. This is the mistake that legislators and political economists have made. God's ownership of land is the primary axiom of their sciences. It is to them what axioms are to the mathematician; what intuitive truths are to the metaphysician, or the law of gravitation to the astronomer. It is the corner stone of social science. When it is left out the social strue-ture must tend to ruin.

Another fundamental truth of the code is, that all land titles are based on God's donation. "The land is mine, for ye are strangers and sojourners with me." God is the host, and we are guests on his land. Our title to land is rather a lease than a fee simple. Only as God grants land have men any righteous claim to it. This truth also is completely ignored by legislation and by political economy. When the blind lead the blind will they not both fall into the ditch?

·A third fundamental principle of the code is that God grants land to man conditionally. When he gives it, he prescribes the purpose for which it is to be used. Nature and reason teach the same lesson. The adaptation of na-ture to supply human needs, teach that this is the end and object of her creation. By its soil, adapted to the raising of grain, its grass, meant to feed cattle, its ores and coal made to supply tools, land proclaims that it was intended to support man and reward him for labor. Reason, equally with revelation, teaches that the earth was made to be inhabited. This truth, perhaps, is not completely ignored by legislation and political economy. But it is very dimly and imperfectly apprehended. Political science will not attain to the wisdom of manhood until it grasps it firmly. It is a maxim of social science. Treatises should be written about it. Every text book should explain it. It is the keystone of the arch of social order. As it has been left out, political economy is merely a heap of polished stones. No wonder that communism grows when the teachers of social science are silent about the first truth of their science. No wonder that property in land is attacked when legislation never speaks of the first axiom that should shape all land legislation. Some may think this is an unjust accusation. Does the law regard land in any other light than as property? Does it distinguish between land and wealth? Does it treat land as the tool of labor? Does it at all discourage the holding of land idle? This truth, that land was made to be used, can not much longer be disregarded.

A fourth principle of the Mosaic code is that land can be forfeited. When not used for the purpose for which God gave it, the rights of the human owner cease. In bitter curse this truth is proclaimed through several chapters. Ebal and Gerizim uttered it. Legislation knows nothing of this fact. Political economy has never heard of it. History has only very imperfectly seen it. Though man ignores it, God enforces it. Working slowly, in and by the laws of national decay, he removes the unworthy tenants from his land, and gives it to others who may better use it, in accordance with the terms of the primeval grant.

A fifth maxim of the code is that land ought to be private property. Almost all the regulations about inheritance, about the jubilee, and the history given in the book of Joshua, assert this truth. There is nothing in the code that favors the nationalization of land, the using of land for public purposes (except what was needed for public buildings) or the ownership of the land by the government. Property in land has been adopted by every code of law, and accepted by all social and political science, and is approved by the moral judgments of the race. In all countries where industry has advanced, private property has been almost the universal rule. When the government has owned the land, there has been tyranny and poverty.

A sixth principle underlying the Mosaic code is that the laws about land and about wealth may wisely differ. Its land legislation is peculiar. We find various rules that apply only to land. There is nothing like them in regard to wealth. It is decreed that land shall not be sold in perpetuity. Every half century it is to return to its owner or his heirs. The law is expounded, and houses in unwalled and Levitical towns must be treated as land and revert at the jubilee. Every seventh year the land is to rest. The tithe of the land is reserved by God for the support of the Levites. A second tithe is to be given to the poor. The gleanings of the field and vineyard are to be left for the widow. The corners of the field are not to be reaped. We do not think that these would be good laws for other countries and nations. We do not think that they are obligatory now, even in Canaan, on the Jews. But they show that in the judgment of the Creator laws about land may wisely differ from the laws about wealth, that the Lawgiver thought the land needed special regulations and prescribed land laws that were peculiar to land.

We are wiser now. Our political science sees no difference between the two kinds of property, land and wealth. Our law treats both alike. It regards the distinction between real and personal property as accidental rather than essential. In real estate it refuses to distinguish between the land which is God's work, and the houses, factories, stores, barns, fences, orchards, etc., which are the results of our labor. As far as possible, the same laws and rules of judicial procedure are applied to both. The tendency in our legislatures and courts is to lessen rather than to increase the distinction between them. Both are taxed alike. If personal property escapes taxation it escapes by evading and not by obeying the law. Land and wealth are treated as if the distinction between them was unimportant.

Is it not possible that the ancient code was right and the modern legislation is wrong? Are there not many differences between them —such differences as require unlike laws and modes of treatment? Both are property, but our titles to land and to wealth differ in two respects. Our title to land is derived mainly from gift. Our title to wealth comes mainly from labor. In buying land we buy what has been given, but in buying wealth (merchandise or houses or goods), we purchase what has been made, and therefore earned by labor. The ownership as well as the origin of the title differ. Our estate in land is limited; in wealth it is unlimited. Our property in land is conditional; in wealth it is unconditional. I would not be understood as teaching that wealth has no responsibilities, or that it is not God's gift. But there is a great and wide difference between what has been given to us and what we have earned ourselves. Wealth comes indirectly from God, through labor. Land is his direct gift. The responsibilities connected with the ownership of land are therefore greater than those connected with the ownership of wealth. The land-owner has duties to the community that the owner of merchandise has not.

The amount of land can not be increased. The quantity of wealth may be greatly, indefinitely increased. Discovery may, and probably will add new area to the domains of industry. Invention may and will increase the utility of land. But labor can not enlarge the earth's surface. It can not reclaim soil from the ocean. To the increase of wealth no limits can be set. Labor may, and probably will, if our civilization is unchecked, multiply the amount of wealth now on the surface of the globe a hundred fold. Land is stationary in amount; but wealth is progressive.

The power of land is abolute; the power of wealth is limited. Land is the absolute necessity of life; without it we can neither live, nor work, nor sleep nor be buried. Wealth is not a necessity of life. Races have lived for generations with very little wealth. Savages have multiplied when their wealth only consisted of a few rude tools and rough clothing. Labor does not depend on wealth; it can create such wealth as it needs. If all the wealth of the United States were destroyed to-day (except what was necessary for the pressing wants of humanity) its houses, stores, factories, barns were burned, its cities, towns and villages levelled, its railroads, telegraphs, tunnels and bridges annihilated, its merchandise consumed, the country would not remain desolate. The people would rebuild their houses, their cities and villages, their railroads, etc.; would replace their merchandise and reprint their libraries. In twenty-five years there would be more wealth in our country than there is today. But labor can not create land. Labor is the creation of wealth and the dependent of land. Not bread, but land is the staff of life; for with land bread will come, but without it existence is impossible. Land is labor's only necessity.

Wealth regulates itself, but land needs regulation. Land endures, but every form of wealth tends to decay. Nature improves land, and ruins wealth. The speculator in wealth must care for his stores, guard them and insure them; but the speculator in land needs no store-houses and no insurance. Wealth is dependent on labor. Land is superior to wealth. The influence of wealth, though very great, and often tyrannical, is limited by the three facts, that it depends upon labor for its preservation, that even with such care it will deteriorate in time, and that labor can supplant it with other wealth. Land has despotic power. The landless must have land at some price, at any price, or perish.

Do not such facts as these intimate that,

while land and wealth are both property, the law should treat them somewhat differently? May not the land laws wisely differ from the wealth laws? The students of social science would do well to desert Blackstone and Adam Smith; to sit for awhile at the feet of Moses. The obligations of the world to the Bible are already beyond computation. To this debt a future age will add a system of land legislation that is founded on truth, and is consistent with the facts of our industrial development.

A seventh fundamental principle of the Mosaic code is that the land-owner owes special duties to society, that land has peculiar obligations. Every seventh year the fields and vineyards were to lie untilled, partly that the soil might rest and partly that the poor might eat. One seventh part of the possible products of land was thus to be sacrificed for the future good of the country and for the support of the poor. We do not read that one-seventh part of the wealth of Israel, of the corn, wine, oil and raiment, was to be given to the poor. We do not think that this would be a good law for our country and climate, and we will not assert that this law was obeyed in Canaan; for these do not affect the point we make, that, in the judgment of the Creator, land has special obligations to society. The gleanings of the field and vineyard were to be left to the poor. "And all the tithe of the land, whether of the seed of the land, or of the fruit of the land is the Lord's; it is holy unto the Lord," to be disposed of by him. The tithe was and is primarily a land obligation. The Mosaic code teaches that the possession of land imposes special burdens on the land owner.

Our codes differ from that of Moses. We impose no special taxes or burdens on land. As nearly as we can, we equalize the taxes on land and on wealth. We do not distinguish between the lot and the house which stands upon it, the fields and the cattle that graze them, the mines and the machinery that work them. We have one rate of taxation for both. Indeed, as we raise the larger part of our revennes by indirect taxes, by imposts, excises and licenses, the weight of taxation falls upon consumption, that is upon labor. Land, instead of being specially burdened, is specially exempt. But there are many reasons why land should bear the burden of government.

A land tax is more easily, cheaply and surely collected, Concealment is impossible and undervaluation difficult. Armies of collectors, assessors, guagers and watchmen could be discharged from governmental employ to devote themselves to production. The expenses of government would be thus greatly reduced, and its machinery would be greatly simplified.

In a land tax, all that is collected of the people is received by the government. It is otherwise with indirect taxes. The merchant charges his customer not only with a profit on the cost of the goods, but with a profit on the import duties. If he pays a license, he raises his prices more than enough to reimburse him. The owner of houses not only collects the taxes, but something additional to pay him for the trouble of collecting them. The owner of a factory raises the prices of his wares more than the amount of his tax. All indirect taxes, and all direct taxes on wealth, are shifted to the consumer; and the consumer pays more than the government receives. But the tax on land can not be shifted. The land-owner who pays it, pays it all to the government.

A land tax cannot check production. Of course such a tax will be proportioned to the value or rent of the land. A tax on the amount of land used might throw land out of use. Such a tax is not intended by a land tax. Most other taxes discourage production. A tariff checks the importation of goods. A tax on houses discourages the building of houses. A tax on orchards would discourage the planting of trees. A tax on cattle diminishes the number of cattle. The taxation of wealth discourages economy and the saving of wealth. The taxation of labor diminishes the efficiency of labor by decreasing its rewards. But a land tax can not diminish the amount of land, or its productiveness. If wisely laid, it will not diminish even the selling price of land.

Other taxes are demoralizing. Personal property can be concealed or removed. A large part of personal property does escape taxation through the prevarication of its owners. Imports are undervalued. A custom house oath has become a by-word. And no remedy for this demoralization of the public has yet been discovered. The importer who does not follow the example of the rogues is placed at a serious disadvantage in the competitions of trade. The merchants who pay the taxes which their competitors evade, can not do business as cheaply or command as large a business. There are no such temptations to fraud or deceit connected with the land tax.

By interesting the tax payers in the economical administration of government, the land tax will purify government. Those who pay the indirect taxes to the government are often opposed to their abolition. They diminish competition. The importer or the manufacturer makes a profit on them. No profit can be made on the land tax. No competition is avoided. It comes solely from the pocket of the land-owner. He will enquire earnestly into its necessity. He will object to paying more than is absolutely required. The land-owners are in almost every country, and certainly in ours, the most influential class in the community. When their self-interest is bound up with an honest and economical administration, we may expect governmental purity.

Nature does more for the land-owner than it does for the laborer or the capitalist. She is good to all. She ripens the farmer's grain. She fattens his cattle. She turns, through steam, the manufacturer's wheels. In a thousand ways she helps all. But she is more generous to land. While labor grows old and feeble, land lying idle improves. While houses fall into ruins and wealth decays, the fertility of the soil increases. To whom much is given of them should much be required.

Society also does more for land. It, like nature, helps all, It increases the efficiency and the rewards of labor. It protects from robbery the wealth of the capitalist. It increases both wages and interest. But it increases rent and the value of land more regularly and more persistently. Wages have unearned increments, as we have seen, and interest also has unearned increments; but the unearned increments of land value are more regular and persistent. Every new-born infant, every immigrant, every invention, every improvement in industry, every reform in government, every railroad, adds to the value of land. Where society gives much she may ask much.

The land is a gift, wealth is earned. Surely what is freely given ought to taxed, rather than what is earned. The land is God's, and the magistrates are his ministers; and it is proper that his servants should be paid out of his estates. So were the Levites, who were the public servants of Israel, paid by the Lord's tithes. The land belongs to God, and paupers are the Lord's poor; should not his bounty supply their wants? The teachings of natural religion are plain. The land is never sick and never weary; can not childhood and womanhood be spared the burdens which the land is so well able to bear? Why should the text-books of the children, the tools of the workman, the medicines of the sick and the coffins of the dead, be made more expensive by indirect taxation or by the direct taxation of factories and machinery, in order that the owning of land may be made more profitable? Is this just, or right, or wise? Modern statecraft places the burdens of society on labor to relieve land. Moses makes land peculiarly subject to them. Perhaps the cause of the difference is that our laws have been influenced by the covetousness of man, while the Mosaic code was inspired by the wisdom, justice and goodness of the Creator.

CHAPTER IX.

THE LAW OF THE TITHE.

The New and True Social Science—The Law of the Tithe—The Language of a Proprietor—Addressed to Individuals—Man's Title to Land is Conditional—Religious Wants of Humanity—The Tithe, therefore, Primeval—Founded on the Creation—The Analogy of the Sabbath—The State can not Enforce it. Note on the Poor Laws—The Glory and Shame of the Church—Will Always be Poverty—Justice Trying to Show Mercy—The Function of the Church is Mercy—An Argument for the Tithe.

The coming generation will build a truer and wider political economy and enact wiser and more just legislation about land. This better science and legislation will be founded on the principles of natural religion and justice which we have found in the Word of God. The first of these is that the land belongs to God. The second is that he gives land to men. And the third is that he grants land conditionally for the support of the race, for the supply of human wants. These principles are illustrated by the law of the tithe.

This law is first explicitly stated in Leviticus 27: 30, in the following words:

"And all the tithe of the land whether of the seed of the land or of the fruit of the tree, is the Lord's; it is holy unto the Lord."

As a moral or religious enactment the tithe does not fall into the plan of our discussion. Of the advantages that come of tithing to the one who tithes we say nothing. The paying of tithes does undoubtedly increase the faith and love of the one who pays them; but this branch of the subject we leave to those writing about the gospel. Our topic is the truths about land taught by natural religion, reason and justice which are clearly exhibited in the Word of God. Because the tithe illustrates these truths we treat of it.

The law quoted above is the language of a proprietor. It is a landlord who is speaking. As a farmer renting his land might say to his tenant: "The fourth of the grain and the "third of the fruit shall be mine." So the Creator declares: "All the tithe of the land, "whether of the seed of the land or of the "fruit of the tree is the Lord's." The tithe is founded on God's ownership of the land. Because the land is his, the tithe is his. His right to the tithe flows from his right to the land. In enjoining the tithe God claims the land.

The law of the tithe is addressed to individuals. It is not an injunction to magistrates or nations. The Word of God nowhere approves of the nationalization of land, of making land the property of the State or of using its rent as a national revenue. It has very much to say of land, much more than the world has imagined, and it always regards land as private property. This law is another illustration of the truth that God gives land to men. It is addressed to individuals, because God gives land to them.

This law also illustrates the truth that God's grants are conditional, rather than absolute, leases, rather than deeds in fee simple. He gives land to men to supply human wants. The first and greatest of these are the moral and the religious. We need virtue more than bread, piety more than wealth, the fear of God more than industrial progress. Where these are all else will come. Where these are not all else will perish. With these, there will be a supply for all mental and bodily wants. Without them there will be a lack of all things. To supply this most pressing want of humanity, God, in giving land, has reserved the tithe. "It is holy unto the Lord."

Man needs to be frequently and regularly reminded of God and heaven, of truth and duty. Man's greatest necessity is the worship of God. To supply this want God has reserved the tithe in granting land to men. There will be no efficient preaching unless the preachers are allowed to give themselves wholly to their work. They can not give themselves to the work unless they are supported. They will not be supported unless there is a fund regularly set apart and appropriated for this purpose. And the Creator, in his land grants, reserves the tithe for this purpose. He gives land to men for the supply of human wants. The greatest of these is the worship of God. This worship needs support. Houses have to be built, ministers are to be educated, ordained, and exclusively employed. Missionaries are to be sent to distant lands. The poor must be provided for. The support that the gospel needs will not be fully and regularly supplied unless there is a fund provided for the purpose. In giving land to men for the supply of human needs, God reserves the tithe to supply man's greatest need. The law of the tithe is primeval.

Let us re-state the facts. Man is a triad; he has a body, a mind, and a soul. His needs are three fold; those of the body, of the mind, and of the soul. He has bodily, intellectual and spiritual wants. The spiritual needs of humanity, the wants of the soul, are the most important. But owing to inborn depravity, selfishness and greed, they will not be supplied unless a fund is regularly provided for this purpose. This fund is the tithe. God gives land to supply human wants; and he has reserved the tithe to supply the spiritual wants of humanity. Thus the law of the tithe is embodied in the very grant of land. It is a condition of the lease by which we occupy the soil. It is a rent reserved by God.*

All the references made in the Bible to the tithe confirm this view. The first explicit mention of it, which we have quoted, does not establish a new ordinance. It refers to it as something well known and already established. Ages before, we find Abram tithing

*We do not think that land alone should tithe. Labor and wealth are also subject to the obligation of tithing, although it is primarily an obligation of land. The land-owner, the laborer and the capitalist are all bound to tithe. But it is no part of our purpose to expound fully the law of the tithe.

and Jacob promising to tithe. Indeed in the wide diffusion of decimal numeration we have an indication of the early existence of tithing. We count by tens, not because we have ten figures, but because in the infancy of the race the tenth was God's. And the law has never been repealed. It does not prohibit any free-will offerings inspired by Christian love. Never was there more need of it than in our own age and country. We have escaped the great evils that flow from State support to religion, only to fall into the evils that come from its non-support. Outside of the cities and wealthier sections the church buildings are shabby and mean, and the ministry poorly paid and discouraged. The Church is a mendicant. Its ministers are often regarded as beggars. Its benevolent operations are always languishing for lack of funds. Our present condition shows the absolute necessity of God's law of the tithe. The State cannot supply the means needed for the spiritual wants of man without injuring the cause of religion. Free-will offerings are not a regular and sufficient fund. The land is given to supply human wants. Man's religious wants are the greatest. The tithe is reserved by the Proprietor for this purpose.

This view of the tithe is supported by the analogy of the Sabbath. When the Creator made man he saw that he needed a regular period for rest and worship. In giving time to men he reserves the seventh day. If God had not sanctified it, selfishness and greed would soon deprive the laborer of the rest-day. The support of religion is as necessary as a day to worship. Man's first day was the Sabbath. The law of the tithe is implied in the first grant of land to man. Both the Sabbath and the tithe are primeval. Both are necessary to man's highest good. Both would perish but for the command of God.

It may be objected that if tithing is an obligation of natural religion and reason, the State should enforce its payment. If this is a necessary result, it would be a valid argument; for the State has, and ought to have, nothing to do with contributions for religious purposes. But it is sufficient to remark that there are many violations of natural religion which the State does not and should not punish. Courtesy is a duty. Anger is wrong, But the State cannot compel courtesy or punish anger. The magistrate, although a minister of God, is human and finite. He has all he can do to preserve public order, to punish offenses that directly affect the public welfare. The State deals with crimes. The punishment of vices and sins it leaves to God.

The tithe is not a maxim of piety, but a duty enjoined by nature, reason and conscience. All should tithe, whether they are religious or irreligious, for the same reason that they pay their other debts. It is honest. The failure to tithe is dishonesty. It is robbery —not of men, but of God. In giving lands to supply human wants, the Creator gave the tenth to piety and charity. To divert it to our own benefit is fraud, and not ordinary fraud. To steal from the causes of religion, intelligence and charity, is the meanest kind of stealing.

NOTE ON THE POOR LAWS.

It is both the glory and the shame of the church that there are in every Christian country poor-houses erected and maintained by the State for the relief of the poor. The Church may glory that she has so widely diffused the principles of humanity that every civilized country lays taxes for the relief of paupers; but she must blush that she allows the State to do the work that she could do so much more kindly, wisely and economically.

There will be poor. Even after the burden of taxation has been removed from consumption, and transferred from poverty to property, after the liquor traffic has been abolished and after the misuse of land, so often connected in the past, with its ownership has been ended, there will still be poverty. Where there is sickness and death, there will be cripples, invalids, widows and orphans. All the poor belong to the Lord; and they should be relieved from the Lord's tithes.

The disadvantages connected with the present mode of relief are numerous. The State's aim is justice, and not mercy. When it tries to give alms, it is out of its province. It does it clumsily and awkwardly. It can do it, as an elephant can thread a needle; but it can not do it gracefully or graciously. It must act by fixed rules. This is right in the sphere of justice, but it is wrong and heartless in the domains of charity. The State can not discriminate between the worthy and the unworthy. It can not give one kind of help to one and another kind of assistance to another, as their different needs require. All it can do is to shelter the houseless and feed the starving. Its refuges from poverty, the poorhouses, are hated and often dreaded by the poor more than death itself. Its relief is often cruel, and always heartless and inconsiderate. It discourages self-respect. It fosters and increases pauperism. It discourages the charity of the Church; for church members are apt to think that when they have paid their poor rates they have done their whole duty to the poor, unless it be to the poor members of their own church or denomination.

The function of the Church is not justice but mercy. She has no inflexible rules. She can adapt her relief to every individual case. She will accompany her gifts with looks of love and words of sympathy. She can bring to the poor the best cure for pauperism, and the best solace for sorrow—the Gospel. She always points upwards.

As Christianity creates the sentiment that leads to the relief of the poor, the Church should administer the funds raised for this purpose. No doubt she would often make mistakes; but State relief makes many more.

One dollar expended by the deacon would go as far as two spent by the overseer of the poor. Where the State makes paupers, the Church, by her active sympathy of individuals for individuals, would restore the poor to self-support and self-respect.

Matters of detail we do not discuss.

The necessity for the relief of the poor is another argument for the primeval origin and natural obligation of the tithe.

CHAPTER X.

THE PROPHETS AND LAND.

Prophets are Inspired Philosophers—The Past the Image of the Present—The Prophets' Teachings About God's Title to Land—About Man's Title—The Old Testament a Treatise on Land Tenure—Isaiah's Woe—Not a Denunciation of Robbery—The Commerce of Blood Forbidden—An Example of it in Isaiah's Age—A Passion for Large Estates—How Much Land May One Own?—Punishment a Natural Result of Wrong Doing—The Iniquity of Sodom—Its Economical Causes, not the Pastoral Life, nor Agriculture, nor Commerce, nor Slavery; but Land Owning—The Landlord's Sins—Pride—Extravagance—Idleness—Debauchery—Contempt for Industry—Was Land Made to Raise Sodoms?—The Evils that Spring From Wealth Diminish Those that Come from Land-Holding Increase.

Note on Land Speculation.—Is It Wrong?—Speculation is Generally Beneficial—Illustration, Joseph—Land is a Commodity—Speculation Does Good—But is More Apt than Other Speculation to Pass into Extortion—And Should Not be Fostered by the Government

In the prophecies of the Old Testament we have God's opinion about human society. In the sacred histories we have a view of God's participation in human affairs. In the prophecies we have inspired observation and philosophy.

It is a common mistake to suppose that

former times were altogether unlike our own. Human nature is always very much the same. The laws of political economy have never varied. The principles of society change very slowly. Nature is the same. The mental and bodily powers of men do not vary greatly. And the amount of knowledge possessed by the people is similar. One age studies one thing, and another age gives its attention to other knowledge; but what is gained in the latter branch of science is lost in the former. The savage studies nature, the civilized man books, but to study books he neglects nature. The social organization and the prejudices and opinions of men change, but human nature remains. The past and the present do not answer to each other as the image in the mirror answers to the reality. The present is not the photograph of the past. And yet there is such a general resemblance that we can study the present in the past. As it was in the days of Christ, as it will be in the end of the world, so it was hundreds of years before in the days of Sodom and of Noah: they were eating and drinking, buying and selling, marrying and giving in marriage.

In the last books of the Old Testament we have accurate pictures of the social and political condition of Judea and Samaria, Edom and Moab, Tyre and Damascus, Nineveh and Babylon and Egypt. These pictures are accurate because inspired. They are absolutely free from the limitations of merely human observation. They give us the judgments of the Creator concerning political and social organization.

We go to the Bible as a book of facts. With its precepts of faith or maxims of piety, we have at present nothing to do. We regard God simply as the Creator. We are looking only for those principles of justice and equity on which all just government and social organization must rest. The prophets were the harbingers of Christ, but they were also the inspired observers of their own age; and as such we come to them for political wisdom. What truths do they teach us concerning land?

They acknowledge a creation and a Creator. In opposition to the superstitious tendencies of their people they assert the sovereignty of Jehovah. They claim for him dominion over all the earth. They maintain that Jehovah is the owner of the land.

They assert also that God gives land to men. "I have made the earth, the man and the beast that are upon the face of the earth, by my great power and by my outstretched arm. and I give it unto whom it seemeth right to me." (Jeremiah 27, 5.)

They teach that this grant is conditional. "For thus saith the Lord that created the heavens; he is God, that formed the earth and made it; he established it; he created it not a waste, he formed it to be inhabited." (Isaiah 45, 18). The land was made, and is given to men, for the supply of human wants.

Malachi, the last of the prophets, asserts the law of the tithe.

But the great political lesson of the prophets is, that land when wrongly used is forfeited. This truth is repeated and reiterated by every one of them in almost every form, not merely in words but by significant actions. It is asserted as a truth, applicable, not only to Palestine, but to every country with which the prophets had to do. It is maintained as a general principle of universal application. If land is misused, its inhabitants will be removed, its owners will lose their property. The heart grows weary in reading the denunciation of the prophets against those who had violated God's primeval covenant with man. Book after book, chapter after chapter—the teaching of this truth stretches out in almost wearisome iteration.

The Old Testament, with the exception of the poetical works, may be regarded as a work on land tenure. Its construction is strictly logical. The creation leads up to the first grant of land to man. In the history of the antediluvians we have an account of the first forfeiture of land. The earth is given afresh to Noah. The historical books are mainly a record of the land grants to various nations, but especially to Israel. And the last part of the Old Testament asserts at much length and with great force and eloquence, that the lands thus bestowed are justly and righteously forfeited if the conditions, on which they were granted are not complied with. In the poetical books also are many isolated references to the same truths.

Two passages in the prophets require careful study. The first is as follows:

"Woe unto them that join house to house, that lay field to field, till there be no place; that they may be placed alone in the midst of the earth. In mine ears, said the LORD of hosts, of a truth many houses shall be desolate, even great and fair, without inhabitant. Yea, ten acres of vineyard shall yield one bath, and the seed of a homer shall yield an ephah."—Isaiah 5: 8-10.

This is not a denunciation of fraud or violence. Isaiah is not an Elijah denouncing an Ahab for seizing the vineyard of a Naboth. There is not a hint of cheating or robbery. The estate is secured gradually. One house after another is bought at a fair price. Field after field is bought of those wishing to sell. But the honest purchaser is threatened with the judgment of God! It is not strange that the ears of the prophet's age were deaf to him. Will the present age listen to Isaiah?

But is his "woe" justified? The Bible does not regulate prices. It allows supply and demand to do this, except in a single case. It forbids the commerce of blood. There are times too sacred for business. Human misery must not be coined into money. Starvation must be relieved, and not bargained with. The one who refuses to rescue a drowning man, except for money, is a murderer, and not a laborer. Thus the Bible does not allow the employer to grind the faces of the poor by giving the very lowest wages that will be taken: for to do this is to make a profit from human misery. So as the rich man's corn is the only resource in famine. "He that withholdeth corn, the people shall curse him." (Proverbs 11: 26.) He who would coin starvation into gold should be cursed. So sacred is this principle that we are not to take advantage of the necessities of others, that the Jew was not even to use them to enforce the payment of just debts. For temporary loans the outer garment of the east was a convenient and customary pledge. But not even to obtain what was due could it be kept over night. (Deuteronomy 24: 13). In the east the corn is ground before each meal, and the millstone could not be taken as a pledge. In the pressing necessities of humanity, business has no place.

Speculation is not condemned by this rule. He who buys corn when it is low to sell when it is high, is as truly a benefactor as the merchant who buys goods when they are cheap to sell them when they are dear. Commerce equalizes the price of goods the world over, and speculation equalizes the price of goods at different seasons. Both services are beneficial.*

The land of Judea was an absolute necessity to the Jew. He could not emigrate, for

*Land speculation has some features of its own, and will be treated of at the close of this chapter.

thrice every year it was his duty to worship in Jerusalem. The houses and fields which the rich had bought were to him what bread is to the starving, or a rope to the drowning man. The purchase of them was a commerce of blood; it was buying the lives and souls of the people. No motive could justify it.

The rich of Isaiah's age had that passion for "grounds," parks and large estates that prevails now. They wished to be placed "alone in the midst of the earth." The merchant prince lives alone in a city square, monopolizing air and sunshine that would give health to hundreds of tenement children. A nobleman enjoys a park that would feed an English village, or depopulates a Scotch county to shoot deer. Other motives for the monopolization of needed land are lower. Speculators hold city lots or country fields to make money. Or, land is bought as an investment. But there is a "woe to them that join house to house and lay field to field" when the land is needed for human welfare. To hold such land is a sin against the Creator, and a crime against humanity. For the land belongs to God. We have it only on lease. The first condition of the lease is that it is to be used for the supply of human wants—not merely for the bodily wants, but for the support of people in such circumstances as will promote their health, intelligence and morality. Land was not made to gratify pride or to display wealth, or to make money out of, or to serve as an investment. To use it, mainly for ostentation, as deer forests, parks, grounds, or as vacant lots, or as a source of income, when it is needed for higher uses, is a violation of the first law of the creation. If land was made to be used as an investment, it should be illimitable; for wealth may increase indefinitely. To hold land needed by population is a commerce of blood.

How much land may one hold without sin? If the population is very scant he may own ten or a hundred thousand acres. If the land is absolutely essential to the support of the population, no one can, without sin, hold more than he can use for this purpose.

Two replies can be made to this statement. It may be said that this is mere theorizing; that there is no way to prevent the undue holding of land. Every one desires more land. The question whether anyone can use more land aright is too intricate for courts to decide. But the single tax the imposition of all the common burdens of society on land, will check the evil or remove it.

The other objection is, that the land-owner does not monopolize his land; he seeks tenants; and rented land will yield as much food as any; and that to own land to rent is using it to supply human wants. The answer to this objection is easy. In creation "the Lord sought a holy seed." Food for the body is the smallest part of the conditions of the grant. Land must be so used as to promote the intelligence, piety and health of mankind. Is the yeoman or the renter the best citizen? Who has the most self-respect, the one who owns his fields, or the tenant-at-will? Who loves his home most—the one who owns it or the one who leases it? It is the common judgment that the ownership of land tends to produce self-respect, love of country, love of home, good order and piety.

Isaiah's "woe" was no empty threat. As he foretold, the houses were desolate, the mansions were uninhabited, and the fields were unproductive. The punishment of sin is not (as men fancy) a marvel, but the natural, inevitable effect of wrong doing which, though often delayed, is sure. Each of the houses that had been joined together might have sheltered a patriotic family, and each field would have yielded a braver soldier to repel Nebuchadnezzar. Joined in one estate they produced an enervated family and the country was conquered. Self-preservation is a law of States. It is essential to the morality, and intelligence and independence of our people and the preservation of our civil liberties, that our citizens should be land-owners.

The other passage to which we call special attention, is as follows:

"Behold this was the iniquity of thy sister Sodom; pride, fullness of bread, and prosperous ease was in her and her daughter; neither did she strengthen the hands of the poor and needy."—Ezekiel 16:49.

The iniquity of Sodom is here described as four-fold; first, pride; secondly, extravagance; thirdly, idleness; and fourthly, a failure to assist industry. We leave it to the preachers to dwell on the moral and religious lessons of the history of Sodom. What political truths can be gathered from its history? It is a common mistake to regard Bible ages as unlike our own. We are warned against this error in the case of Sodom by Christ himself. "In the days of Lot, they ate, they drank, they bought, they sold, they planted, they builded," as they are now doing. The principles of human nature, of political economy and of social growth and decay, were the same then as they are now. Like effects were produced by like causes then; and like causes will produce like effects now.

What cause or causes produced the iniquity of Sodom? What will produce at once pride, extravagance, idleness and lack of helping the poor? It was not the pastoral life, for this does not support extravagance or allow idleness. Agriculture also requires industry and gives employment to the poor. Trade may support extravagance, but it discourages pride and idleness, and it gives employment to the needy. Slavery there was in Sodom; but while slavery may foster pride and deprive the needy of work, it does not support extravagance or permit an "abundance of idleness." The argument of Helper's "Irrepressible Conflict" that slavery was unprofitable, was not and could not be answered. Rich Southerners there were before the war, but their riches came from cotton, or from rice, or from sugar, and not from slavery. They owned the only regions where some of the world's greatest staples were raised. Their wealth was caused by "rent." The slave-holder who did not have the help of a rich soil or a special product, lived frugally and worked hard. The hardest workers on a plantation that did not have special advantages of soil or climate were the master who was the merchant, store-keeper, book-keeper, apothecary, overseer and judge of the village, and the mistress who was the overseer of the women, the teacher of the children, the nurse of the sick, who saw that the food was properly cooked and that the wool and cotton were rightly carded, spun, woven and sewed. There was often an abundance of idleness on a Southern plantation, but it was not in the big house.

One cause remains—rent. Although Ricardo had not stated the laws of rent they were in full force. "Rent is the share of "wealth which the exclusive right to the use "of natural capabilities gives to its owner." Its law has been stated thus: "The rent of land "is determined by the excess of its produce "over that which the same application can se-"cure from the least productive land in use." To illustrate: If Lot could raise three heavier sheep in the well-watered paradise of Jordan, with the same labor as two lighter sheep on the hills of Canaan, he could and would give one sheep for rent to the owner of the plain. If he could fatten two head of cattle on the plain while he could only fatten one on the hills, one would be rent. Or if Lot would not do it some one else would. The sheep or bullock would be received by the land-owner without labor. As population increased on the plain and in the hills, as poorer land was grazed, rent would increase, and the land-owner would receive a larger proportion of the product without toil. It is possible that the men of Sodom may have had business as well as agricultural rent, for the commerce whose profits afterwards built Petra and Palmyra, may have passed through Sodom. Rent was the economic cause of the four-fold sin of Sodom.

Pride comes from the undue ownership of land. Except in the gentry it seems out of place. "Purse-proud" is a reproach. But family pride, pride of birth—the deepest of all pride—seems fitting to the land-owner. The landlord's son soon sees that he fares differently from other boys. They eat coarser food and wear coarser clothes. The boys of the merchant and the manufacturer quickly learn that their advantages come from the store and the mill. To the landlord's heir, they seem rather a tribute of nature, an acknowledgment of his inborn superiority. The adulation of servants and the society of those taught in the same school, confirm his early impressions. The distinction between the classes is accepted as an ordinance of nature and of God. The pride of rank nourishes those virtues that are necessary to the maintenance of rank, courage, courtesy and honor. This is all that can be said in its favor. In other respects it is evil, and only evil. It leads to contempt for labor and for laborers, to indifference to the sufferings of the lower classes, to insolence toward man and impiety toward God.

Another sin caused by the renting of land is extravagance—"fullness of bread." The money has come without labor, and it is spent without thought. "Easy come, easy go." As it required no toil to produce it, it is squandered. In societies, where the undue ownership of land needed by the people has created a public sentiment, the extravagance of landlords is commended. A nobleman owes it to his rank to spend money lavishly. The extravagance of the rich, it is said, is good for trade. The saying is false. The money that is squandered, if used to promote production, would add to the comfort and happiness of all. Extravagance is as injurious to the community as it is to the one who wastes his money.

A third result is idleness. The "prosperous

ease" is the special badge of the gentry. In England the Duke's son, who engages in trade, disgraces himself and his family. But industry is necessary to the welfare of body, mind and soul. Health, intelligence and piety are almost impossible without regular employment. The indolent are subject to bodily, mental and moral diseases. The gout is an aristocratic disease. Insanity claims the indolent as its victim. The rich forget God. Labor develops the body and expands the soul—not the drudgery of the street-car driver or the factory operative, but remunerative, hopeful labor. Mere "exercise" will not answer the purpose. Living on rents is "prosperous ease." He who reserves a toll from others for the use of the bounties of nature has an "abundance of idleness." The capitalist is kept busy. If his wealth is in trade, he must sell and replenish his stock ; if in ships, he must engage crews and cargoes ; if in machinery, he must keep it moving ; if in houses, he must find tenants and repair and rebuild them. The business man is busier than his hands. There are connected with the use of capital risks that occupy the mind. There are no risks about land. If unused, it improves. If population is growing it increases in value, and makes its owner a profit without thought on his part. The landlord simply receives and spends the rent. God did not create land to support sloth.

It may be said that this argument condemns bonds and stocks. The bondholder's only tool is the scissors he uses to cut off the coupons. But there is a great difference. The bonds or stocks or mortgages are the result of labor, the evidences of indebtedness or of part ownership created by labor. The bondholder's title is absolute. But the land-owner is only a lessee. He did not make his land. He holds it on the condition that he use it for the highest good of himself and others.

After labor comes rest. After industry comes the enjoyment of what has been earned. If the work and wages have been honest, the enjoyment usually will be beneficial. After the landlord's abundance of idleness comes "fullness of bread," an extravagance that only does harm, a profusion that injures brain and body. As no appetite has come from the prosperous ease, rare food and wines are sought to tempt the sluggish desire. There is such an indulgence in wine, in meat and in sleep, as sickens the body, stupefies the mind and deadens the conscience. Wearied with pleasure, the victims of *ennui* seek excitement in debauchery. So it was in Sodom, and so it has been elsewhere. It has been the experience of every age, that abundance, unearned by labor, tends to debauchery. There was in Sodom, as there has been in other countries, a dissolute aristocracy. Lord Macaulay thus describes a London custom that reminds one of the Biblical account of the destruction of Sodom:

"It was a favorite amusement of dissolute young gentlemen to swagger by night about the town, breaking windows, upsetting sedans, beating quiet men and offering rude caresses to pretty women. Several dynasties of these tyrants had, since the Restoration, domineered over the streets. The Muns and Tityre Tus had given place to the Hectors, and the Hectors had been recently succeeded by the Scourers. At a later period arose the Nicker, the Hawcubite and the yet more dreaded name of the Mohawk."

If the vice of London, Paris and New York is now more decorous and demure, it may yet be deeper and more shameful.

The fourth part of the iniquity of Sodom, is a failure "to strengthen the hands of the poor and needy." The renting of land does not help industry. A landed aristocracy on the contrary contemns labor. Rent constantly tends to reduce both wages and interest. The number of people increase, the amount of land does not. Where population is sparce there is a competition between land-owners who want hands or tenants. But as population becomes dense, the competition is between those who must have the use of land at some price, at any price, or die. All else can be dispensed with. Land is the absolute necessity. The farmer must have a field, the merchant a lot, the family a little plot. Houses are not necessary; if the use of land can be obtained a cave can be dug, or a tent or shanty erected; but without land the merchant's goods perish and the laborer is idle. In all other commerce the question is: How much will the purchase give? But in the traffic about land, as the demand for land increases, the question is: How much *can* the renter pay? As laborers increase in number and in skill, all other commerce tends to become freer, for as industry develops there is a larger stock to select from, and the cost of production is diminished: but the demands of land become more rigorous. In other trades the customer may or may not buy; in this he must buy, or emigrate, or die. Whether the land is in few or in many hands, the landless become more and more dependent. More and more of the earnings of labor must be paid for the use of land. till there is barely enough for the body and none at all for the mind, hardly enough for food, and none for books or for charity. The industry of Sodom, the owning of land to live off of its rents, debases the landlord, and degrades the laborer. It not only deprives the laborer of the virtues that come of the possession of land, love of country and love of home, but it constantly tends to reduce him to a meager and precarious subsistence.

Did Jehovah create the land to raise Sodoms on? Is that use of land, that always and everywhere tends to produce pride, extravagance and idleness in one class and penury and servility in another, in accordance with the laws of the Creator? Are the land laws that sanction such a use of land right? Can the landowners, who use their land to feed their pride, to supply their extravagance, or to maintain them in idleness, expect to be acquitted by the Creator in the day of judgment?

The prophet calls Sodom the "sister" of Jerusalem, which was to his age what London and New York are to our age—the centre of gospel light and evangelistic activity. The men of Sodom were not naturally worse than other men. Sodom was the natural result of the laws of political economy and the principles of human nature. Given the same conditions in any country among any race, and Sodom is the inevitable result, except for the grace of God. The conditions are the land-laws of England or of the United States, a small country, a dense population continually growing, and no emigration. Rent will take more and more, wages will get less and less. There will be wretchedness in the cottage, and pride, luxury and debauchery in the mansion.

The evils that come from the unequal distribution of wealth lessen while those which come from the undue ownership of land increase. Riches take to themselves wings and fly away, but land remains forever. The heir of the capitalist must inherit some of his skill and industry, or the capital will not be profitable: the landlord's son needs neither skill nor industry, and indeed, he despises both. The store and the factory will be unproductive, unless the owner has industry and judgment. Rents increase however idle and dissolute the landlord may be. Wealth decays; land increases in value. If these evils are to be abated or removed, the State, civil government, society must interfere. And it can abate and remedy these evils without any violence, without diminishing the value of land, without injustice to any. All that the State needs to do to remove the dangers that threaten us is to impose its taxes more justly and righteously.

NOTE ON LAND SPECULATION.

Is speculation in land morally wrong? Is it inconsistent with the purposes for which land was made to hold land out of use in order to obtain a larger price for it? This is a difficult question. On the one hand there are the great evils that result from speculating in land, but on the other hand there is the general desire of those who are building up a new place that the land should be held by as many as possible.

Two things are sure, that speculation generally is beneficial when not carried too far, and that when carried beyond a certain point it does great harm. There is no difference ethically between the merchant who buys articles where they are cheap to sell them where they are dear, and the speculator who buys goods when they are low to sell them when they are high. Both equalize the price of commodities. Both are a help to the producer and to the consumer. Both are helping to sustain population by paying to the producer a better price, and by selling to the consumer at a lower price. Both may pass the proper limit. Both may oppress the poor. Both may coin human necessity into gold. Both may pass into robbery. It may be impossible to draw the line between lawful profit and extortion In both commerce and speculation, there is such a line.

The difference between the two does not depend upon the amount of gain. We may regard Joseph in Egypt as a speculator in grain. There was in his case no deception or fraud of any kind. Every time he appeared in public it reminded the people of Pharaoh's dream and the approaching famine. In spite of the warning, the people did not provide for the years of dearth. Joseph had the control of the granaries which had to feed Egypt and the surrounding countries for seven years. A great problem confronted him. How should he make the food last? If he charitably distributed to all as much as they wished, the same improvidence that had neglected to provide for the famine out of the abundant harvests would soon waste his stores. If he tried himself to decide how much each Egyptian and each foreigner needed, he would be imposed upon and the provisions would not last. The only way he could "preserve life" was to advance the price of the grain. And as he bought the land of Egypt with his grain, it is plain that he must have made an enormous profit. No doubt it seemed a great hardship to many an Egyptian family that he asked so much for it. But the corn needed the protection of value. It was the best plan—probably the only way—to insure its economical use. Joseph was justified in charging such a price as would make Pharaoh's corn outlast the famine. More than that would have been extortion.

Land is a commodity. It is bought and sold. The owner is sometimes compelled to sell. The landless want to buy. As the speculator in wheat advances the autumn price and reduces the spring price, so the land speculator equalizes the price of land. As the speculator in wheat by advancing the price in the fall prevents wheat from being wasted, so the land speculator aids in bringing land to its highest use. A speculative land value is a protection to land. It keeps shanties from being built on city lots. It keeps farm houses from mineral lands. Thus it saves the builder and the miner the expense of buying useless buildings, and contributes to the opening of mines and the erection of suitable houses. An illustration occurred in western North Carolina ten years ago. The mountain tops were nearly valueless. It was found that two or three crops of high-priced tobacco could be raised on the soil, after the trees were removed, before it was washed away. It was the only way the owners could make a profit out of the steep land. After a short time the fertility was entirely exhausted. These steep mountain lands ought not to have been ploughed. A speculative land value would have preserved the timber on these mountain tops, and have kept the soil when the trees were removed as pasture for cattle. As speculation in grain preserves it for use in the succeeding spring and summer, so land speenlation preserves nature, to be used in after years.

Land speculation, however, is more apt to cross the line that divides trade from extortion, than speculation or commerce in wealth or goods. These regulate themselves; land speculation does not. The one who holds wheat, or hats, or cloth, for an advance in price, has to take care of them, to house them, to watch them, to insure them. Land takes care of itself; needs no housing or watching or insurance. Wheat, or hats or shoes (wealth of any kind except, perhaps, curiosities) deteriorate in value and in usefulness if kept too long. Land does not decay. If the speculator or the merchant asks too much for his goods, a new supply can be made in the course of a few months or a few years. Land cannot be manufactured. The land speculator may indeed drive the people away by prices that are too high, but this is a remote danger. The speculator in goods will after awhile have to compete with the manufacturer. The speculator in land fears no competition. And our government imposes a lighter tax on unused and unimproved land. The power of wealth is very great, but it is after all a limited monarchy. The power of land is an absolute despotism. It is the first and greatest of all human necessities. With it all else can be produced; without it nothing can be made, for without the use of land we can neither work nor live nor be buried. In other commerce the question is, "how much is the buyer willing to give?" In land speculation and in the renting of land, the question tends to assume the shape, "how much is the purchaser able to give?" The ownership of land is tyrannical. For such reasons speculation in land is very often extortion and robbery.

The government evidently should not specially foster and encourage it, as it now does, by imposing a lighter taxation on unimproved land than on improved land. Equal taxation will allow land speculation, but will check extortion.

CHAPTER XI.

THE BIBLE AND LIBERTY.

Liberty, the Bible's Gift to the World—It Teaches Two Truths—First, Magistrates are God's Ministers—Secondly, They are Appointed by the Consent of the People—Illustration from Church Government—Ignoring either Truth, Liberty is Destroyed—Despots "Dei Gratia"—Mob Law—The "Social Contract" Theory—It is not True in fact—Destroys the Reverence due to Government—Cannot Give to Government due Authority—Logically Leads to Despotism—The Acceptance of the Bible Doctrine Limits the Power of Government—Guards the Right of Revolution—Explains the Nature of Government—And States its Object—The Great Danger of our Country—Our Only Hope.

For civil liberty the world is indebted to the Bible. Constitutional government is its gift to men. Although civilization and philosophy flourished in the classic ages, constitutional government in any large country was unknown. There were free republics, but they were of limited extent and short duration. Absolute government was the rule then, as it is now in heathen countries. Only where the Bible has taught the people the truths of political justice, is constitutional freedom possible.

With Christianity we still have nothing to do. We go to the Bible, not because it proclaims the gospel, but because it teaches the political truths that underlie all just government, both in Christian and pagan countries. There is not and can not be such a thing as a Christian political government. Christ's kingdom is not of this world. The Church and the State have different aims, and use different means to attain them. The Church seeks the conversion and sanctification of all the people. The State seeks their worldly welfare. The Church uses moral suasion. The State employs force. The Church can not convert men by force. The State can not repress crime by moral suasion. The strength of the Church is the power of the keys. The weapon of the State is the sword. The two are mutually independent. When the distinction between them is obscured, and the Church aims at political objects, and the State at religious ends, one or both suffer. This book is a political and not a religious inquiry. It refers to the Bible only for the principles of political justice.

The Bible teaches two truths about civil government. First, it asserts that the magistrate is God's minister, appointed by God, deriving all his authority from God, and responsible to God for the exercise of it. Secondly, it asserts that the power is given to the magistrate only by and through the consent of the governed "The powers that be," alone are ordained of God. Only the governments that have the consent of the governed are or can "be." The very existence of the government depends upon the consent of the people. They are very many, the rulers are very few. They have the strength, the wealth. Their consent may be expressed or implied. It may be sullen and silent, or joyous and noisy. It may be manifested in hereditary loyalty or by the ballots of the citizens. But without this consent no government can exist. It need not be universal. Probably no government was ever unanimously approved by its subjects. Few have had the hearty and cordial approval of even three-fourths of the people. The approval of the women and children has always been inferred from that of the male citizens. The precise amount of approval has not been and can not be exactly stated.*

* The mode in which power is given to rulers has an influence on legislation, The judgment of the people. and not that of the rulers, (of the majority and not the minority) should dictate the laws. The conscience of the community is the standard. Of course there is danger of error as in all things that are finite and human; but it is better to have imperfect laws that are approved and enforced, than better laws that are neglected.

These two truths, that God appoints the rulers, and that he appoints them through the consent of the people, are the two fundamental principles on which constitutional liberty rests.

The connection between these two truths is illustrated by church government. The power of the keys is given to the officers of the Church, but it is given to them through the election of the people. Christ gives to the Church officers the power to admit applicants to the sealing ordinances or to reject them if in their judgment they are unworthy; but this power he gives to them only through the suffrages of his people.

Heathenism is ignorant of both these truths. Rulers have frequently claimed the honors due to God. Nebuchadnezzar expressed the thought common to them when he said: "Is not this great Babylon which I have built for the royal dwelling place, by the might of my power and for the glory of my majesty?" In polytheism, where hero worship prevails, it is not easy for supreme rulers to acknowledge that they are merely servants of God, deriving their power from God, and responsible to God for its exercise. Humility is a grace that springs from the seeds of Bible truth, and flourishes least in royal palaces. And when the first fact, that authority is derived only from God, is unknown, the other truth that it comes only through the consent of the people is also unknown.

If either one of the two truths is exclusively dwelt upon, civil liberty will suffer. When the first truth that authority comes from God is alone acknowledged, despotism results. Kings have claimed to rule absolutely "Dei gratia," by the grace of God, and have been crowned by the ministers of religion. It was and is a monstrous perversion of the doctrine of natural religion made known to us in the Bible.

But in our age and country there is more danger of the tyranny by the majority than of tyranny by a monarch. And the despotism of the majority may be worse than royal despotism. The chief opponent of the truth about civil government, in our age, is the theory of the social compact. According to this theory government originated in a contract The people saw the disadvantages arising from the want of government, met together, established a form of government, and endowed it with authority. All since born, by accepting the advantages of social order, have tacitly agreed to the original social compact. By this theory the authority of government is derived, not from God, but from man. It is admitted that this original social contract is a fiction; but it has been thought a useful expedient to explain the nature of government, and a good foundation on which to raise civil freedom. But it only recognizes one side of the true doctrine, viz: that the authority of the rulers is conveyed to them through the consent of the governed. Logically it leads to oppression and tyranny.

The theory is not true in fact. No nation ever started in this way. It is admitted to be merely a fiction. Fictions are not to be admitted into science, and least of all into social science and political economy. It is more than a fiction, it is an impossibility. No body of people ever existed that could make such a contract. As children and parents, husbands and wives, relatives and neighbors, they were already under obligations to each other. The theory supposes that those who formed the compact were mutually independent. Human beings never did and never could exist in such a state. As men are mutually independent of each other commercially, they may form commercial companies. But socially they are not independent. By birth the child is subject to government. The parent and husband is clothed with authority by the Creator. Government precedes society.

The theory robs civil government of the reverence due to it and needed by it. According to this theory the authority of govment is the same in character as that of a manufacturing company or a debating club. These derive their power from the agreement of their members. It is wrong for their members to violate their rules, because it is wrong for them to break their word. The authority of the State is higher. And it may be added that many of the citizens of any country have never expressly promised to obey its laws; and that none of those native-born were ever in an independent position in which they could reject its authority.

From no social contract can the State gain the authority it needs. It needs the right to tax, to imprison and to kill. I may indeed agree to give it the right to take so much of my own property as it may need, for public purposes; but I can not give away my neighbor's property. It may be necessary that some of his property should be used for public purposes; but for me to take it from him is simply robbery. And the consent of others will not make it right. Henry and Richard and John cannot of right take James' property for public purposes without his consent. If they do it by force they are a band of robbers. But since God gave James all his property he may justly take it away. And he delegates the power of taxation to the rulers. "For this cause we pay tribute, also."

In regard to imprisonment, the case is still stronger. For I have no right to agree to surrender my own freedom; and much less can I contract away the liberty of others.

But the case of the sword is strongest. John has no right to kill James; and he can not delegate to others the power he does not himself possess. James may deserve to die; but this will not change the fact. James has no right to promise to let John kill him. And John and Richard and Thomas have no right to kill James. The right of life and death belongs only to God, and to those to whom he delegates it. The necessary powers of government can be derived from God alone.

But the greatest objection to the theory of the social compact is that it logically leads to despotism. Blackstone begins his exposition of it with the following sentence:

"The only true and natural foundation of

society are the wants and the fears of individuals."—Commentaries I., p. 47.

It follows that society may justly do whatever is required by the wants and the fears of individuals. Mr. Henry George has taught hundreds or thousands that the wants of individuals require the confiscation of rent. According to Blackstone, such confiscation, if it will promote the general welfare, is "in accordance with the only true and natural foundation of society." If the confiscation of capital, as others teach, would be advantageous to the community, it would be right. If the safety of the State is the highest law, then it is right for the State to lie, steal, murder babies, burn heretics, if these things will promote the public prosperity. If the confiscation of the unearned increments of wages, as has been the custom in many lands, approves itself to those having authority, this will be just. There is no iniquity which can not be justified by the social contract. It is unwritten, vague and indefinite. Its only interpretation is the will of the majority. It gives to the majority absolute power, unrestricted by the fear of God or by the conscience of man.

Against this atheistic theory we assert that government is the ordinance of God, established by the Creator when he said to the mother of mankind, "Thy husband shall rule over thee." We assert that rulers are God's ministers, appointed by God, deriving their authority from him and responsible to him. The mode of their appointment is through the consent of the governed, which alone can make government stable. By proclaiming this truth, which is as old as Genesis, and is frequently stated in the Old Testament, Paul became the father of constitutional government and civil liberty in Europe and America.

For the consequences of this truth are weighty. Every society that accepts it establishes thereby a constitutional government. It renounces the right to pass any laws contrary to the principles of righteousness, established by the Creator, and made known to us by nature, reason and conscience. It promises that the laws shall be in conformity with the Creator's will. The ruler who claims to reign by the grace of God admits an authority greater than his own, to which his own acts should conform. The benefits which come from such acknowledgments and promises are great.

It follows from this truth again that no government has any right to make any law opposed to the will of God. Any such law is null and void, and is not binding on the conscience of the subject. The powers of government are limited by its origin. It can only do that which nature, conscience and reason allow should be done. If it makes laws opposed to the principles of natural religion, as, for example, that parents should kill their children, or that men should blaspheme God, such laws are unconstitutional. As ministers of God, the legislators had no authority to make them.

Government, as a servant of God, is not only forbidden to make unjust laws, but is also required to make good laws. It is bound, in its sphere, to carry out the purposes of the Creator, as these purposes can be gathered from reason, nature and conscience.

Again it has no authority to punish such acts as are innocent by the laws of natural religion. It can not impose new obligations on the conscience. In matters commonly called indifferent it must consult with righteousness. For example, it should forbid the storing of gunpowder in crowded cities. But the municipal law does not make it wrong. If there were no law it would still be wrong; for where population is dense the storing of large quantities of gunpowder needlessly endangers life. A municipal law requiring the merchants to erect powder magazines on Broadway in New York city would be unconstitutional, null and void. In morals and in government there is nothing morally indifferent. Every act is either right or wrong. Government in all its actions, as the servant of God, is bound to be governed by truth and justice. But when it is a question whether any act is right or wrong, the judgment of the individual should yield to the judgment of the community, as expressed in its legislation.

The right of revolution is guarded by the true doctrine. For rulers are only God's ministers as they are appointed by him through the consent of the people. If the people have not or do not consent to the reign of any emperor, king, or governor, he is not God's minister, but is an impostor, and has no right whatever to the authority he profanely claims. Dethroning the tyrant is obedience to heaven. As the amount of consent or approval needed to legitimate government can not be stated accurately, so it is impossible to say how much discontent will justify rebellion. This is a better foundation for the right of revolution than that offered by the theory of the social compact, which bases it on the desire to promote the public welfare. Rebellion is right, according to the common theory, when the evils of resistance are less than the evils of obedience. As war is a necessary incident to rebellion, it is right to kill to promote the public welfare, to do evil that good may result—a Jesuitical doctrine. According to Paul's doctrine that only existing governments—governments that have the consent of the people—are ordained of God, the revolutionists dethroning a tyrant are as much the ministers of God as the police officers who arrest a burglar. The tyrant is a sacrilegious pretender. The sword, the power to kill, is given by God to the rebels. Of course, there is danger of error, as there is in all moral questions. Only a very general disapproval of the rules can justify rebellion.

The true doctrine explains the nature of government. Formerly all over the world, as now in heathenism, the power of government was regarded as a private possession. Rulers regarded their authority, as land-owners now regard their exclusive dominion over land, as something to be used for their own benefit and personal glory. The Bible has established the doctrine that a public office is a public trust, to be used, not for the advantage of the offices, but for the benefit of the public. In the days of Nero, government needed to be reformed. In our days of invention, of progress, of growing riches and poverty, the dominion over the earth which we call landed property, needs to be reformed. The Bible has cured the evils of despotism, not by abolishing government, but by reforming it. And the Bible will cure the evils that spring from land holding, not by abolishing the private ownership of land, but by reforming it.

The true doctrine of government makes clear the true object of government. As the minister of the Creator the magistrate is to labor, in his own province, for the end which God had in view in creation. This end is stated by Malachi. "He sought a holy seed." The magistrate, government, or society, "God's minister" is to make such laws and ordinances as will permit and assist men to lead holy lives. The father of American liberty thus states the true object of government: "I exhort therefore, first of all, that supplications, prayers, intercessions be made for all men; for kings and all that are in high places, that we may lead a tranquil and quiet life in all godliness and gravity." This is the first and only main, chief end of civil government—the securing to all the opportunity of leading quiet and godly lives.

The protection of property is not a main or chief end of government, because it was not God's aim in creation and is not his object in providence. The State should protect property, but this is not its main object. It should protect property, but not for the sake of the property, but for the sake of the people. Does God care as much for property as for people? Is it a main object of his providence to defend riches? Does he teach us, either by revelation or by nature, that the acquisition of riches is the primary object of life? Do not the Bible, reason and observation warn us against the undue pursuit of property? Does God secure property to its possessors? Has he not impoverished nations, desolated countries and destroyed cities for the sake of promoting the moral influence of the people? If civil government is God's ordinance, is it not bound to accord with God's government. The magistrate should protect property, in order to secure to the people the opportunity to lead quiet and godly lives; but this is only a secondary object of government, like coining money, carrying the mails or supplying water or gas.

Our American government is compelled to

face a great foe. The increase of poverty threatens the very existence of our civil order. The barbarians that overthrew the Roman empire came from without; we are breeding our own barbarians within. It is not safe to commit the destinies of an empire to dependents. Beggars for work are not safe electors. Tramps are not good citizens in a republic. A presidential election may be decided by bribery. The personal independence of our citizens is the material out of which our ship of State has been constructed. This was the common condition of our people before the war; for we had then no tramps. When the stout planks of individual independence are supplanted by the rotten wood of great fortunes and hopeless poverty, the ship of State will founder. What will survive the wreck none can tell. We can not go back. We can not derive any relief from our anxieties from preceding centuries or other countries; for the industrial development of our age and country is unexampled. Our cities grow like mushrooms. Invention succeeds invention. Trust follows trust. The production of wealth is exceedingly rapid. But this production does not bless all classes alike. The rich are growing richer and the poor poorer. Poverty, the dependence of workmen on employees, the separation of society into classes, advances more rapidly.

In our extremity the Bible is our only political salvation. The truths about land and about civil government, which the Creator has made known to us in his inspired Word, alone can save us. Rejecting these truths we shall be hurried on, faster and faster, in the maelstrom of our material and atheistic civilization, into social destruction.

CHAPTER XII.

GOD'S GOVERNMENT AND GOD'S LAND.

The Answer now Easy—The Facts Re-stated—The Illegal Use of Land by the Liquor Traffic—The Government Bound to Encourage the Right Use of Land—By making every Land-owner a Judge—The Single Tax—Will Discourage the Unproductive Possession of Land—Is Just—Is Seemly—Will Relieve Poverty—Will Encourage Industry—Will be a Great Economy—Will Purify Politics—Will Simplify Government—Will Favor Morality—Will Increase Patriotism—Objections—"Unequal"—"Rent Can not Support the Government"—"The Single Tax will Destroy Land Values"—"Will Injure the Farmer"—"Difficulty of Assessing Land"—"Taxing Improvements"—The Real Objection—An Appeal to the Justice of Americans—The Regeneration of Earth.

What are the duties of governments in regard to land? The "land question" must be answered. We cannot escape it. The growth of poverty will destroy our liberties, overturn our form of government and finally destroy our civilization. What can society do to check this growth? Unless we meet the question social destruction awaits us. We have come to the answer by slow steps, through truths undoubted by any Christian and almost indisputable. It will now be easy to give a correct answer. Before doing so let us recapitulate the steps we have taken:

I. The land, the natural opportunity to labor, belongs to God.

II. It is and ought to be, the whole race being judge, property.

III. The title of the land-owner is indisputable.

IV. Land in densely populated countries needs the protection of value.

V. The nationalization of land, or the confiscation of rent by the State, necessarily creates despotism and increases poverty.

VI. God gives land to individuals.

VII. The gift is not absolute, but conditional. The land-owner cannot do as he pleases with his land. He must use it for the support of population in such circumstances as are favorable to their physical and moral well-being.

VIII. If he fails so to use it, he forfeits it, and loses all title to it.

IX. As land is a monopoly, it is subject to peculiar laws.

X. The land-owner has special burdens in supporting the government.

XI. Civil government is the ordinance of God.

XII. The power to tax is derived from God.

XIII. As the servant of God, government must obey the will of the Creator, as made known to us by conscience, reason and nature.

From these truths we can deduce safely the answer to the question which American citizens must answer, and answer before many years pass.

Since government is the ordinance of God, it is morally bound to conform to the laws of the Creator. Its only safety is in obedience.

The first law of the Creator is, that land is to be used for the support of population: of a moral, intelligent and healthy population. The State, as God's minister, is to enforce this law.

When we look about us, we see a large portion of land, God's land, devoted to the production of an article that causes more poverty and more crime than anything else. Such a use of land is plainly unlawful. It is a violation of the condition on which land is bestowed upon men. The government, the Creator's agent, is bound to see to it that the terms of the grant are complied with by the occupants of the land. The plain duty of government is to extirpate the traffic in intoxicating beverages. This can not be done by high license or by local option, that treats the traffic as a matter that is indifferent in its nature. It can only be done by prohibition, national and state, with prohibitory officers, national, state, county and municipal, to enforce the law. This traffic should be prohibited by the government, not simply because it is immoral, nor because it is injurious, nor because it is politically corrupting. These are all good reasons for suppressing it. The reason we urge is different. The distiller, brewer and saloon keeper use land, God's land, not to benefit people, but to impoverish and debase them. Such a use of land is unlawful. The easiest way to prevent it is to prohibit the traffic. The farmers who raise grain for the distillers and brewers, are also guilty of misusing their land. As the grain is bought in the open market, the only way to prevent this misuse of agricultural land is to forbid the trade.

Government, as God's ordinance, is not only bound to prevent the flagrant abuse of land, but also to encourage its right use. As the agent of the Creator, it is its duty to see that the ends of the creation are carried out. This duty can not be performed directly. If it tried to judge the conflicting claims of those who wished to occupy land, it would never be done. Every farmer wants another field. Every coal operator would like another mountain. Every owner of a saw mill would like another forest. Every citizen wants a larger garden. To decide whether these different classes could wisely and beneficially use more land, would be an endless task. It would be impossible to draw with distinctness the line that separates right and wrong land speculation. But where the State can not judge, it can engage the citizens to do it, each in his own case. Where society can not decide, its members can. Government can employ as many judges as it has land-owners; and each one will consider his own case carefully, and generally decide it wisely. If any one has land which he is not using beneficially to the public and profitably to himself, he will want to sell it. Each one will wish to retain only so much land as he can use in accordance with the primeval law of creation for the supply of human wants.

The plan by which the State can accomplish this result is to remove all taxes from consumption and production, from labor and wealth,* and to impose all taxes necessary for the economical administration of government, on land—not on the area of land, but on the

* We have always tried to employ these terms, land, rent, labor, wages, wealth, capital, value and utility only in the technical meanings we have assigned to them.

value of land. Besides the tax on land the government may wisely tax monopolies. Those to whom are granted special and exclusive privileges may well be taxed. As the owner of a monopoly always charges all that the traffic will bear, all that it is profitable to charge, he can not transfer the tax to the community by raising his charges without injuring his own business. A tax on ostentation is also a direct tax, but it has never been imposed in our country, and it can produce so little revenue that it is not necessary to dwell on it. An income tax also cannot be shifted, but it is inquisitorial.*

The effect of the single tax on land values will be to discourage the unproductive holding of land. Men do not like to pay taxes. They avoid the paying of taxes by every means they can. When the land-owner finds that his

* When all taxes on industry have been removed I would like to see the poll tax extended and increased. The advantages of this tax are many. It gives every eitizen an interest in the government. It guards their self-respect. When devoted to the support of the public schools, it increases the attendance. Poor people feel that they have paid for them, and are more willing to send their children. They want to get back the value of their money. It is well for every one to have a personal pecuniary interest in government. But as long as the present mode of taxation continues; as long as production is hindered, consumption diminished, and industry is discouraged, by taxation, the poll tax ought not to be increased. It ought rather to be abolished.

land is taxed and that all other property is untaxed, he will sell the land that he is not using productively and invest the proceeds in property that is free from taxation. The owner of two vacant city lots will sell one and build a house on the other, to escape taxation. The farmer who has more fields than he can plough or graze, will sell the fields that he can not use, to supply human wants, and buy more stock or better machinery, or build himself a better house, so as to avoid the tax collector. Thus land speculation will be very much checked. When land is offered for sale, at much below its present or prospective value, it will still be bought on speculation; but it will not be kept idle for an indefinite period. No one will wish to hold land that is not used for production. Only the rich can afford to hold valuable land idle, and they will soon grow tired of paying taxes.

The great argument for the single tax, to my mind, is that it is right, and that nothing else that has been proposed will secure the just and righteous use of land. The argument is conclusive. The land was made by God to supply human wants. Civil government is an ordinance of God and is bound, in its sphere to see that the purpose of creation is carried out. The single tax is the only practicable plan to prevent the unproductive holding of land. Of all plans of taxation, it, and it alone, is in accord with creation. All other plans of taxation are the invention of human ingenuity. The single tax alone harmonizes with the purpose of creation.

It is also in accord with the truth about civil government. The ruler is God's minister, The land is God's land. The ruler (kings. queens, presidents, governors, lawmakers, judges, constables, policemen, soldiers, sailors and all others needed to preserve the public peace)—needs support while attending to the work to which he is appointed by God. What is more seemly than that he should receive his support from the rents of God's land?

The single tax largely removes the taxes from poverty on to riches. The poor will still be taxed, but they will be taxed more lightly than ever before No plan is practicable that will altogether relieve poverty from taxation. The widow and the orphan will still be taxed on their home if it occupies valuable land. But they will be released from the taxes they now pay on nearly everything they eat or wear from the cradle to the grave. The crushing weight of taxation is one main cause of our poverty. For our present taxes, tariff, licenses, taxes on personal property and on houses, factories, etc., are chiefly taxes on consumption; and the poor must consume or die. The tax on mills and machinery increases the cost of manufactured goods. Import duties add to the price of foreign commodities and domestic goods of a like kind. Licenses and taxes on capital increase the prices of things that are sold. Why should the clothing, the food, the books, the coffins, and even the plain tombstones of the poor be taxed when such taxation is altogether unnecessary?

Our present taxes are chiefly taxes on consumption. The consumer pays the import duties, the taxes on houses, machinery, merchandise and capital. Most of our taxes are indirect, and are transferred from one to another until paid by the one who uses the articles. A tax on consumption is a tax on the necessities of the people. Our wants, and not our abilities, are taxed. Taxation passes over property to collect the expenses of the government from the needs of the people. Such a mode of raising revenue is unjust. Property, riches, prosperity, should pay the ruler, and not need and want.

Taxes on consumption press heavily on parents. With no greater income than others, their wants, their consumption, is far greater. They have several mouths to feed, several bodies to clothe and house, several minds to educate. Political economy gives them no more wages or interest or rent. But the State in taxing consumption exacts more from them. The father who rears a godly family of children has done society a service and ought to be rewarded rather than fined.

Taxes on consumption are unduly severe on workingmen. It takes as many yards of cloth to make him a suit as it does the millionaire, and he wears out his clothes faster. He eats more than the rich man. But on every commodity, the richest and the poorest are taxed alike. Surely the rich should contribute more than the poor to the expenses of government.

Our present taxes are taxes on labor. They discourage industry. They do this in three ways. They are taxes on consumption. As the cost of things consumed increases, the demand for them, that is the demand for labor, diminishes. Because the State adds to the price of things consumed, the opportunities of labor are curtailed. But the tax on consumption also increases the cost of production; for consumption is necessary to production. The increased cost of things produced limits the market for them, and thus again diminishes the demand for labor. All taxes on wealth are really taxes on labor. If a workman economizes and accumulates capital, taxation fines him for his economy ; if he builds a house, the tax assessor punishes him for his industry ; if he saves money and buys a team, the State fines him in taxation for his frugality ; if he imports a cargo of valuable goods he is fined for his enterprise ; if he opens a mine the assessor rebukes him for trying to supply his fellow men with coal or iron. Some one has said that he who makes two blades of grass grow where only one grew before, is a benefactor of the race. The tax assessor does not think so, but makes him pay for his temerity. It can not be denied that our present tax discourages industry and frugality.

The tax on land value is free from these objections. It does not and can not add to the price of things consumed. It does not make production more expensive. It does not rest on the needs of the people, but comes out of the rent of land. It does not press heavier on parents than on bachelors. It does not discriminate against the poor. It hinders no work. It fines no one for industry, economy and accumulation.

On the other hand the single tax will encourage labor. It will remove all the discouragements which indirect taxes impose upon labor, and it will open new opportunities to labor. Land is labor's great and only necessity. Without land labor is impossible, with land labor can employ itself. Tools can be made. Capital can be saved. The single tax will give labor easier access to land. It will do this, not by destroying or diminishing land values, but by making those who hold valuable land unproductively more ready to sell at a fair price.

The single tax has other advantages. It will be a great saving to the people. They now have to pay not only the taxes but a profit on them. Indirect taxes are shifted on to the consumer; but in their passage they grow. When population is increasing, even the tax on houses is an indirect tax; and the house-owner charges his tenant more than enough to repay the tax to him. The same is true of the manufacturer and the merchant. The importer has to make a profit on the duties he pays as well as on the foreign cost of his merchandise. Import duties also raise the price of domestic manufactures. Far more is paid to the home manufacturers than to the government. The State receives a part, and only a small part, of what a protective tariff costs the people. The land tax will be all paid to the government. The cost of collecting such a tax will be less than the cost of collecting other taxes. The people will pay no profits on the taxes to middle men. The whole loss of the people will be the gain of the government.

The single tax will purify politics. It will do this in several ways. It will reduce taxation to the lowest point consistent with the efficient administration of government. Now there are large interests that successfully oppose any reduction of taxes. Protected industries bitterly fight tariff revision, however necessary it may be. The importer who makes a profit on the imports he pays is not urgent for the abolition of the duties on which he makes a profit. The internal revenue, by increasing the amount of capital necessary to engage in business, diminishes competition; and the distillers, brewers and manufacturers of tobacco oppose any reduction of the taxes which they pay. The single tax will destroy the strong opposition to low taxes. No one will be interested in keeping up taxes.

On the contrary all the tax-payers will be interested in lowering them. The owners of valuable land will support the government, and what they pay to it they can not collect from their fellow-citizens. They will wish to pay as little as possible. They will earnestly enquire into the expenditure of their money. They will demand, and will secure economy in governmental expenditure.

Government wil lbe much simplified .A large part of its energies is now employed in colleeting its revenues. The temptations to fraud and deceit in our present system of taxation are so great that armies of spies have to be employed. Under the single tax there will be no temptation to fraud and no possibility of deceit. Land can not be concealed or carried away. The valuation of land is a much easier task than the assessment of houses, jewels, horses, factories; than the watching the ports to see that no dutiable articles slip through; than the inquisition into private affairs to find out how much money and stock each one has. A single receiver in each district will take the place of the armies of assessors, collectors, inspectors, gaugers and watchmen that are now employed. The expense of collecting the revenue of the State will be similarly reduced.

The single tax will improve political morality. By our theory of taxation personal property ought to pay equal taxes with real estate. It is notorious that it does not, that taxes are only paid on a small proportion of the personal property of the people. Taxes are systematically evaded by concealment, that is, by fraud. This evasion is corrupting. The merchant is constantly tempted to undervalue his imports. Business men are likewise tempted to understate their capital. If they do not they are at a disadvantage in the competition of trade. In this respect also the present system is disadvantageous to the poor. The millionaire's bonds are easier concealed than the mechanic's tools or the farmer's team.

Direct taxes are more favorable to public spirit. A tax that is unnoticed does not awaken as much inquiry or create as much interest in governmental affairs as a direct payment to the revenue collector. In this respect the taxes that cannot be shifted on others, the land tax, the income tax, and the monopoly tax, excel all others.

The single tax will thus secure to politics a part, at least, of the time and energy that is now squandered in pleasure-seeking. When land-owners pay the taxes they will be greatly interested in political questions. Society will thus obtain the assistance of the leisure and education that is the blessing of hereditary riches.

The single tax can not in any way hinder production. Land is not manufactured. The land-owner cannot annihilate his land and destroy its value. All other taxes except the four direct taxes, the taxes on land, on monopolies,* on incomes and the poll tax, do tend to hinder production, to make the supply of human wants more difficult, and to create poverty. The land tax is in thorough harmony with the purposes of the creation.

The advantages of the single tax are almost indisputable. What objections are urged against it?

The most common objection is that it is unequal and unfair. The rich man who owns no land would escape taxation. Three answers to this objection refute it. The first is that the

*It is possible that a tax on monopolies might prevent the building of new railroads, or the erection of gas works, etc. But the danger seems to me remote and uncertain, and I let the text stand. Income taxes, if they embraced the income of the poor, might be oppressive. The objection to income taxes are many and serious, and I hope that they will never be revived in the United States.

present mode of taxation is far more unequal and unfair. A large amonut, perhaps the larger part, of personal property, does not pay taxes. But the larger part of our revenues are raised by taxes on consumption, that is by taxes not on our abilities, but on our necessities. Such taxes are essentially unjust. The second reply is, that no system of taxation can be devised that will make all contribute their exact and equal proportion. The third answer is that the rich man must use land, and will probably use valuable land. If he does not he will leave more land for the use of others.

Another objection is that rent, the annual value of land, is unable to pay the expenses of government. I have not prepared any statistical answer to this objection. Figures do lie, and statistics often deceive. I prefer rather to call the attention of the reader to several well known facts. Farmers renting farms on shares pay one-fourth, one-third, one-half of the crops, or even more, for the use of the fields. A part of this is for the use of the house, barns, fences and other improvements, but the larger part of it is for rent of the land. Will not one-fifth part of our agricultural products support the government? A family living in the city on a moderate income pays one-third or one-fourth of it for house-rent,* and one-third or one-fourth part of this house-rent is rent. Will not the one-twelfth part of all the money spent in the larger cities to support families support the government? A large part of the expense of carrying on business is store-rent, and perhaps one-half of this store-rent is true rent. There can be little question that the rents of all the lands in our country would support our governments, national, state, county and municipal, a dozen times, if they were econonically administered.

A contrary objection is that the single tax would destroy land values. If true, it would be a valid argument against it. Land needs the protection of value wherever there is a dense population. Valueless land will soon be barren. As soon as land ceased to be property, to have value, it would be ravaged. But this great governmental reform would not even diminish the value of land. It would on the contrary greatly increase it. All that makes a city or a country a better place of residence, or a better place to do business, raises the value of land. Free trade, the removal of the barriers which prevent our doing business

* This compound word "house-rent" is not "rent" as we use the word.

with other nations, from selling to them what we can most cheaply produce and buying of them what they can produce most cheaply, would increase the value of our land. The removal of all the checks to production or to accumulation, which we call indirect taxes, or taxes on wealth, would increase land value. The greater public spirit, the higher tone of personal honor among our people, would make our country a pleasanter place to live, and increase the value of land. Even if the people should, after awhile, decide to lay taxes, and buy all railroads, telegraphs, telephones, gas-works, water-works, and all other works that are monopolies this, if done prudently, would increase the value of land. As the building of a railroad raises the prices of adjoining land, so a better and more public-spirited management of the railroads would increase land values. As regular mails make land more desirable, so a better management of telegraph and telephone lines would add to land values. If the laying of water and gas pipes increase the value of city lots, a less annoying management of gas- and water-works would add to their value. Justice, truth and righteousness are profitable, and they will increase the value of our American soil.

It is not proposed that our modes of taxation should be changed suddenly or violently. There will be a long discussion. Then, little by little, taxation will be gradually shifted from consumption, from the coffee of the widow, the text-books of the orphan, the clothing of the poor, on to land. The land-owner need not fear that the blessing of the community will be a curse to him. As the country prospers, as poverty disappears, as production is unchecked, his land will become more and more valuable.

Another objection is the fear of the American farmer that the land tax will impose the weight of taxation upon him. He deserves sympathy. His labors are poorly paid. His boys leave him for the city. His house is mean. His enjoyments are few. His work is hard. But the land tax will be a benediction to him. It is the emancipation of our agriculture. Now the burdens rest very unfairly upon the farmer. He is compelled to sell what he makes in the world's market and to buy his goods in the American market—to sell cheap and buy dear. In the taxation of his personal property he is treated unfairly. None of it escapes taxation. Concealment is impossible. All his neighbors know what stock he has. But the personal property of the city merchant, and the bonds of the millionaire almost escape taxation. The single tax will change all this. The farmer will buy in the cheapest market in the world. His house, barn, fences, tools and stock will be untaxed, His fields will be taxed no higher (perhaps lower) than the unimproved land that joins them. And the taxes will not be on acres but on value. Many city lots will pay a higher tax than his whole farm.

Another objection might be made that the assessment of land would be unequal in different cities and counties. The assessors, to relieve their neighbors, might assess the land too little. This is a real difficulty in the taxation of real estate. Boards of equalization do not remedy it. But it is much easier to value land than it is to assess land and houses. General rules could be adopted. Lots in cities of a certain size could be assessed in proportion to their nearness to the business or residence center, etc., at so much a foot. The same rules would apply to the whole country. Agricultural lands could be valued according to their ability to produce crops and their nearness to market, etc. Very little would be left to the judgment of the assessor. The work would be mainly a question of ascertaining facts. And as land values change slowly, it would be sufficient to make an assessment once every five years.

Another objection is that in real estate it is impossible to distinguish the value that comes from labor from the value that comes from nature, to say how much of the value is improvements and how much is land. To tax the improvements is to discourage land-owners from improving their land. The difficulty is a real one. The State can not do exact justice. Much labor is imbedded in the soil, so that it cannot be separated from it. Many improvements are permanent. The fields have been cleared, the stumps removed; rocks have been buried, ditches have been cut and roads made. But because it may be impossible to avoid taxing some labor, ought all labor to be taxed? The difficulty might be obviated. It might be enacted that permanent improvements should not be taxed for thirty-three years. Such a law would not discourage industry. The laborer would have the free use of the fruits of his industry for a generation. And it would be no hardship to include the labors of previous generations among the natural advantages of the soil.

The real objection to the single tax is not often stated. It transfers taxation from poverty to property. It is a tax that can not be evaded and that can not be shifted. Property naturally objects to the transfer. Land-owners and all who hope to be land-owners may be expected to oppose it. If they will consider the matter calmly and reasonably their opposition will vanish. The single tax will not abolish riches. It will not decrease the value of a single city lot or country acre. While relieving the poor, it will not hurt the rich. In freeing production from the restraints by which it is now hampered, the single tax will reduce the cost of all commodities, increase the purchasing power of money and add indefinitely to the comforts of the rich. It is just and right, It is in accordance with the plans and purposes of the Creator. Property may at first resent the proposal to place the whole burden of taxation on rent; but when it examines the question quietly and deliberately it should joyfully accede to it. This book is an appeal to the justice and conscience of the class which has had and will always have most influence in the community, those who own wealth and land. The author has faith in his fellow-citizens. May they be guided to a wise and happy conclusion of the problem which they are now compelled to face.

How shall we abolish poverty? Intemperance is one cause of poverty, and the prohibition of the liquor traffic will prevent much poverty. The taxation that checks production, hinders exchange, and discourages labor is another cause of poverty; and the single tax will prevent the poverty that is caused by taxation The keeping land idle and unproductive while labor has no opportunity to work is another cause of poverty, which the land tax will remove. Other causes of poverty can not be affected by political methods. Only Christianity can regenerate the world. The gospel of Christ is the only means through which his prayer can be answered: "Thy kingdom, come, thy will be done on earth as it is in heaven."

CHAPTER XIII.

THE FUTURE OF EARTH.

An Independent Enquiry—And Yet Related to the Subject of this Book—The Common Idea is Unfounded—Grounds of Hope—God's Object in Creation—Nature's Effort to Free Herself from the Bondage of Sin—Our Own Desires—Unlimited Land Grants—Bible Promises—The Resurrection—Redemption—General Scope of Scripture—The Certainty of the Main Argument of this Book Illustrated by the Uncertainty of this Enquiry—The Future of Earth—Piety and Patriotism.

What will be the future of earth? This enquiry is certainly an interesting one. Perhaps it does not strictly fall into the plan of this work, and yet it is intimately connected with it. Social science has to do with the present and the immediate future. But this is an inquiry into the remote future. Political economy, the science of society, is founded on natural religion, on the principles of justice that must underlie all good and stable government. But in an inquiry into the future of earth we must go, for light, to Revelation, to Christianity. Natural religion can give us little information. The foundations of social science are (or should be) justice and righteousness. Our anticipations for the future of the earth must rest on redemption—on faith and hope.

And yet though this enquiry is not a part of the main argument of this book (which has been completed) yet there is a close connection between it and the subject which we have discussed. Our treatment of land will depend upon the view which we take of it. If we regard it as our everlasting home we will think of it as something very dear and precious; but if we look on the earth as a school where we are only to spend a few years, and which we are to leave when our spiritual education is completed, to go to our true home, our views of it will be much lower. Boys abuse their school-rooms. But men embellish their homes. If we regard the earth as the true home of our race, we will do all we can to beautify it. If the land, the surface of our globe, is the paradise of immortality, it is something holy, almost sacred. The unlawful use of it is a species of sacrilege. The one who uses land to curse, instead of to bless his fellow men, is like the money-changers in the temple who were driven forth with a whip. If the earth is the footstool of God, and the everlasting abode of all his earth-born children, to abuse it is like buying and selling in the holy place.

The common idea is that we are here only for a time, that when our probation is ended, we are removed to another place, and that at the consummation of all things the earth will be annihilated and the saints, clothed again in natural bodies, will be translated to some higher and nobler sphere. Such is the common belief of the Church and expectation of saints.

Such a belief has no foundation in revelation. The passages that seem to teach that the earth will be annihilated, when carefully studied, teach that it is to be purified. The difference between annihilation and purification has not been noticed. The earth is to be destroyed, but this destruction is not annihilation. As the old world was destroyed by water in the days of Noah, so is the earth to be destroyed by fire at the last day. But as the destruction by water was not final, so neither will the destruction by fire be final. As the earth was purified by water, so is it to be purified by fire. As it continued after the purification by water, so it will endure after the purification by fire. This, rather than annihilation, is the true meaning of those prophecies that are quoted for the total and final destruction of earth.

But when we leave a few particular passages and look at the general drift of Scripture, there can be little doubt as to its teaching.

The object of the Creator in creation has been one of the main themes of our book. That object was to support a holy and happy population. "He made the earth to be inhabited," not by the ungodly, but by the virtuous. In creation "he sought a holy seed." If the earth is finally destroyed at the close of the present dispensation, will the plans and purposes of the Creator have been fully and perfectly fulfilled? In the ages that are past, the majority of the race have been irreligious and unbelieving—in a word, they have been ungodly (not godly). The servants of God have not been holy, but they have often been misled by their ignorance, by their passions and by the bad example of others. An apostacy is foretold still in the future. We repeat our question: If the world is annihilated at the day of judgment, will the purposes of its creation have been fully answered? Satan's purpose was to make it the abode of sin; God's to make it the abode of holiness. If it is destroyed finally will it not be, at least seemingly, the triumph of Satan?

Nature confirms this view. The argument is finely stated by Paul in Romans. Nature does not willingly submit to the disgrace of sin. Death is the wages of sin; and nature quickly hides the graves and purifies the corruption within. Wars spring from lusts; but nature covers the battle field with flowers. Greed and indolence impoverish the soil; but nature, if allowed, again enriches it. Selfishness and carelessness pollute the rivers with sewerage; but nature purifies the waters. She dissipates the smoke and stench which large cities throw into the air. She pulls down the hideous structures which are erected by parsimony; for the law of beauty is usually the law of permanence. By ten thousand acts nature shows her abhorance of the dominion of sin, and expresses her desire for deliverance from it. The whole creation is groaning and travailing to be delivered from the bondage of corruption. Nature is subject to this bondage, but it is not a willing subjection. She is a slave earnestly looking for emancipation. She is eagerly waiting for the liberty of the sons of God—that glorious time when the design of creation will be fully carried into execution, and the earth will be filled with a holy population.

Our own instincts agree with the teachings of nature. We are an earthly race. We love our native land. We desire to remain here. Death is terrible because it takes us from earth. After the resurrection we will need some material globe to dwell on. Why should the saints be forever banished to Venus or Jupiter or some other world? None other will ever be "home" to our race. Nature does not willingly submit to the bondage which we have imposed upon her. She is ever striving to fit herself for the abode of the good. Why should they not be allowed to live in their own home-planet? Nature is looking forward to brighter and happier days; as we have shared in her bondage, why should she not share in our glory? The human father consults his children in fixing the place of their abode. Will the Heavenly Father do less? His earth-children will always prefer the earth. Here they gave themselves to Christ, and labored for his glory and the good of others. No other place will have the same associations and recollections. If permitted it may be pleasant for them to visit other worlds; but the earth will be their home.

In this book we have studied the truths that God gives land to men. Some of these grants were unlimited in duration. Canaan was given to Abram and his seed "forever." The word is repeated again and again. The grant is endless. The irreligious Jews. have forfeited it, but does it not still belong to those who have complied with the terms of the grant? Why should the necessary purification of earth, which is to take place at the day of judgment, interfere with this gift? Human deeds are irrevocable. Are God's grants less so? But would not the annihilation of the earth necessarily terminate the possession of the land of Canaan by Abram and his seed? For their sins their rights are temporarily abrogated, but they are not destroyed. Heaven and earth shall pass away, rather than one jot or tittle of the law shall fail. May not heaven and earth endure to secure the fulfillment of the law?

Similar promises are made to others. "Honor thy father and thy mother, that thy days may be long upon the land which the Lord thy God giveth thee." Filial honor no doubt tends to promote long life But have no children who honored their parents died young? Have all lived to old age? Or shall the promise of the fifth commandment be broken? It is a specific promise. A long existence in Jupiter or some other place will not be a fulfillment of it. "The meek shall inherit the earth." Are all the meek land-owners? On the contrary, in our past social organization, have not land-owners especially lacked meekness? Will not the promise of the Psalmist and the blessing of Christ be carried into effect?

The doctrine of the resurrection confirms our hope for earth. For those who again wear flesh and blood will need some solid place in which to live—some globe resembling earth if not this planet. Why should it not be earth? Can those to whom our hope seems fanciful give any good reason why the saints should not dwell on earth when it has been purified?

The redemption strengthens our hope. "Where sin abounded," shall not grace "abound more exceedingly?" Christ is called the second Adam. As the sin of Adam cursed those who are Adam's, so the righteousness of Christ blesses those that are Christ's. As the sin of Adam brought a curse upon the soil, the land, the earth, will not the righteousness of Christ bring to it a blessing and a benediction? The redemption is full and complete: will it not benefit earth? It redeems the bodies of the saints from death: will it not free their home from the curse?

Not on isolated texts do we base our argument for the permanence of earth, but on the general scope of Revelation. As this subject is not essentially connected with the object of our book we will not go into any exposition. We make only two remarks. There is hardly a psalm or a chapter of prophecy to which this belief does not give a more vivid meaning. It will also end the long discussion between the premillenarians and the postmillenarians; for the differences between them are very small, if we believe that the raised saints will dwell on earth after the day of judgment with their incarnate King, when those who have forfeited their title to earth by their persistent rebellion have been forever banished from it.

Whatever may be thought of this argument for the permanence of earth, it does not affect our argument on the land question. This chapter is based on the obscure references of Scripture. The previous chapters were founded on detailed history, legislation and prophecy. The Bible is largely silent about the future; it is full and explicit about present duties. All the Old Testament, except the poetical books, is a treatise on land tenures, The truths that we have stated in previous chapters about land are not exclusively and especially Bible truths. They are the teachings of nature and reason, of justice and philosophy, of conscience and history. The political economy of the twentieth century will acknowledge them as fundamental principles, and will wonder that previous ages did not see them. The duties and debts of land are very plain, however vague may be our hopes. But hope strengthens duty. If we look for the regeneration of earth we will labor more diligently for its reformation.

If—we emphasize the "if"—if the earth is purified and not destroyed by the final conflagration, what will be its future? There will be no sin on the globe. All evil and evil-doers will have been banished. All the effects and consequences of sin (except the saints supreme love to Christ) will have disappeared. The bondage of corruption, to which nature has never submitted cheerfully, will be ended. God's primal law about land will be fully obeyed. The earth will be replenished with the holy and good. There will be no dreary wastes. The hum of human happiness and the laughter of human joy will be heard everywhere. As there will be no more sin there will be no more poverty, or death, or sorrow, or tears or pain. The earth will be fully subdued. Every building will add beauty to the landscape and every road grace to the view. Mountains and rivers will no longer be barriers to human intercourse. And man will be lord of all. No inferior creature, if such there are, will resist or fly from the reign of love. The whole earth will be a garden of Eden, a paradise of God.

Home and heaven are nearer akin than we think. Rejecting Christ we lose both, accepting him we save both. Patriotism and piety are but two names for one virtue. The impious are unpatriotic, banishing themselves forever from their native land, while the pious, if our hope is not too presumptuous, will always live in their own country. Our love for our own homes and for our own country should make us walk humbly with our God.

APPENDIX.

PROOF TEXTS.

The four truths that this book asserts are: first, that God is the original and ultimate proprietor of land; secondly, that he gives land to men; thirdly, that his grants are conditional; and fourthly, that civil government is the ordinance of God, and is therefore, in its own sphere, bound to see to it, so far as it is able to do so, that the conditions of God's land grants are complied with.

Below are references to the proof texts sustaining three of these truths. The doctrine that the State is an ordinance of God has long been familiar to the Christian world; and it has not been thought necessary to adduce proof texts for it. In the first division are texts that assert that Jehovah is the creator, texts that ascribe to him the blessings of nature, and texts that declare him the owner of earth. In the second division are texts declaring that God has given land to the Jews and other nations, and texts that acknowledge the private ownership of land. In the third division are texts that base commands on the ownership of lands, and texts declaring that land has been forfeited. The second and third divisions overlap. It is impossible to draw any sharp line of distinction between them. All God's grants of land are conditional; and when the condition is not stated it is implied. In the fourth division are texts that throw light upon the future of land.

Many of the texts are obscure references to the truths established in this volume. But such indirect references have value in confirming truth.

Bible students will prefer to study the texts for themselves in their connection. The careful study of the Word of God will convince any unprejudiced thinker that the Bible does teach the truths stated in this book.

The references are to the Revised Version.

It is not claimed that this is a complete list of all texts throwing light on the land question.

ABBREVIATIONS.—*Ch.*, chapter; *psm.*, psalm; *v.*, *vv.*, verses; *passim*, everywhere; *etc.*, surrounding verses; *ff.*, following verses; *f.*, first part of verse; *m.*, middle of verse; *l.*, last of verse; *cf.*, compare.

I.

GOD OWNS THE LAND.

Genesis, ch. 1, passim; ch. 2: 1–6; ch. 8: 22; ch. 14: 19, 22; ch. 17: 8–9; ch. 19: 24–25. Exodus, ch. 19: 5; ch. 20: 11, 24. Leviticus, ch. 25: 23. Deuteronomy, ch. 9: 28; ch. 10: 14.

Joshua—The entire history of the conquest of Canaan proves that God has the right to give land—ch. 2:11.

I. Samuel, ch. 2: 8; ch. 12: 18. II. Samuel, ch. 21: 1. I. Kings, ch. 17: 1; ch. 18: 1, 31; ch. 20: 28. II. Kings, ch. 19: 15 l. I. Chronicles, ch. 16: 26, 31; ch. 29: 11 m., 12, 14 l, 15 f. Nehemiah, ch. 9: 6.

Job, ch. 5: 10; ch. 9: 5–8; ch. 12: 15; ch. 34: 13; ch. 38: passim; ch. 39: passim; ch. 41: 11 l.

Psalms, 10: 16 l; psm. 24: 1–2; psm. 29: 3–9; psm. 33: 6–9; psm. 50: 12; psm. 65: 6, 9–12; psm. 74: 17; psm. 90: 2; psm. 95: 4–5; psm. 100: 3; psm. 104: 5, 10, 13, 14, 24, 28; psm. 108; 7–8; psm. 115;

15; psm. 121: 2; psm. 124: 8; psm. 135: 7; psm. 136: 5–9, 25;psm. 146: 6; psm. 147: 8–9.
Proverbs, ch. 3: 19–20; ch. 8: 26–29; ch. 30: 4.
Isaiah, ch. 5: 1–6; ch. 6: 3 l; ch. 14: 25; ch. 19: 25; ch. 27: 10; ch. 40: 12, 28; ch, 42: 5; ch. 44: 24; ch. 45: 12, 18; ch. 48: 13; ch. 51: 13; ch. 54: 2, 5; ch. 66: 1.
Jeremiah, ch. 5: 24; ch. 10: 11–12; ch. 14: 22; ch. 16: 18; ch. 17: 3; ch. 27: 5; ch. 32: 17; ch. 51: 15–16.
Ezekiel, ch. 16: 16, 19; ch. 20: 40; ch. 29: 3, 9; ch, 32: 23–24; ch. 36: 20 l; ch. 45: 1.
Hosea, ch. 2: 9. Amos, ch. 4: 13; ch. 5: 8 l. Jonah, ch. 4: 6 f. Habakkuk, ch. 3: 9 l. Haggai, ch. 2: 8. Zechariah, ch. 12: 1.
Matthew, ch. 5: 35. Luke, ch. 12: 6, 24, 27. John, ch. 1: 3. Acts, ch. 4: 24; ch. 14: 15; ch. 17: 24.
Romans, ch. 4: 17 l; ch. 9: 21; ch. 11: 36. I. Corinthians, ch. 10: 26. II. Corinthians, ch. 4: 6 f. Colossians, ch. 1: 15–17. Hebrews, ch. 1: 2–3, 10; ch. 2: 10; ch. 3: 3–4; ch. 4: 3-4. Revelation, ch. 3: 14 l; ch. 10: 6.

II.

God Gives Land to Men.

Genesis, ch. 1: 28–29; ch. 2: 15; ch. 4: 16; ch. 9: 1–17; ch. 10: 5, 25, 30, 32; ch. 11: 8–9; ch. 12: 7; ch 13: 14, 17; ch. 14: 7, 16, 18–21; ch. 17: 8; ch. 21: 25, 30; ch, 23: 4–20; ch. 24: 7; ch. 25: 9, 10; ch. 26: 3–4, 18–22; ch. 27: 28, 39; ch. 28: 4, 13, 15; ch. 33: 19; ch. 34: 21; ch. 35: 12; ch, 36: 43; ch. 47: 4, 6, 11, 19–20, 24, 26–27; ch. 48: 4, 6, 21; ch. 49: 25; ch. 50: 5, 13, 25.
Exodus, ch. 6: 4, 8; ch. 20: 17; ch. 22: 5, 6; ch. 23: 20, 23, 27, 28, 29, 31, 33; ch. 33: 1–3; ch. 34: 11.
Leviticus, ch. 11: passim; ch. 14: 34; ch. 25: 13; ch. 27: 16–24.
Numbers, ch. 10: 9; ch. 11: 12; ch. 13: 2; ch. 14: 8, 12, 16, 23. 24, 31, 40; ch. 15: 2; ch. 18: 20–21, 24; ch. 20: 17–21, 23–24; ch. 21: 22, 31, 35; ch. 24: 18; ch. 26:

53; ch. 27: 4–11; ch. 32: 5, 18–22. 33. 41–42; ch. 33: 54; ch. 34: passim; ch. 35: 1–8: ch. 36: 3, 7–8.

Deuteronomy. ch. 1: 8, 25, 38–39; ch. 2: 4–5, 9, 10–12, 19–23, 24, 31–32; ch. 3: 3–20; ch. 4: 1, 21; ch. 5: 21; ch. 6: 23; ch. 8: 17; ch. 9: 1, 4. 6, 28; ch. 10: 9; ch. 19: 14; ch. 31: 3, 7, 20, 23; ch. 32: 8, 49, 52; ch. 33: 18, 23; ch. 34: 4.

Joshua—The whole book illustrates thc truth that God gives land to nations, families and individuals—ch. 1: 3, 4, 6, 13, 14, 15; ch. 2: 9, 14, 24; ch. 6: 2; ch. 8: 1; ch. 9: 24; ch. 11: 16, 23; ch. 12: passim; ch, 13: 1, 6, 14, 15, 23, 24, 28, 29, 31, 32, etc.; ch. 14: 1, 3, 5, 9, 13, etc.; ch. 15: passim; ch. 16: passim; ch. 17: passim; ch. 18: 6, 11 ff; ch. 19: passim; ch. 21; passim; ch. 22: 4, 7, 9, 19; ch. 23: 4; ch. 24: 4, 8, 13, 30, 32, 33.

Judges, ch. 1: 2, 3; ch. 2: 1; ch. 6: 9; ch. 11: 12–24, 26; ch. 10: 1, 10. Ruth, ch. 4: 3, 6.

I. Samuel, ch. 8: 12, 14; ch. 12: 8; ch. 22: 7; ch. 25: 2: ch. 27: 5–6; ch. 30: 4. II. Samuel, ch. 7: 10; ch. 9: 7, 10; ch. 14: 16, 30–31; ch. 16: 4; ch. 19: 29–30, 37; ch. 24: 21, 24.

I. Kings, ch. 2: 26 f., 34; ch. 4: 25; ch. 8: 53; ch. 11: 18; ch. 21: passim, vv. 1, 2, 3, 4, 7, 15, 18. II. Kings, ch. 5: 26 l; ch. 8: 3, 6; ch. 13: 23; ch. 17: 24; ch. 18: 32.

I. Chronicles, ch. 1: 19; ch. 4: 10, 23, 28 ff., 40–41; ch. 5: 9–10, 11–16, 23; ch. 6: 65–81; ch. 9: 2, 16, 35, 38; ch. 11: 5; ch. 21: 15 l, 18 l., 22–25. II. Chronicles, ch. 3: 1 l.; ch. 6: 25–31; ch. 11: 14; ch. 20: 7, 10–11.

Nehemiah, ch. 5: 3–5, 11, 16; ch. 9: 8, 22–23, 35–36; ch. 11: 3 m., 20 l.

Job, ch. 12: 23; ch. 15: 19; ch. 22: 8; ch. 36: 31 l.

Psalms, 8: 6–8; psm. 16: 6; psm. 44: 2–3: psm. 61: 5 l; psm. 78: 54–55: psm. 80: 8–10; psm. 105: 11; psm. 107: 36; psm. 115: 16.

Proverbs, ch. 12: 11; ch. 22: 28; ch. 23: 10; ch. 24: 30; ch. 29: 19; ch. 31: 16.

Isaiah, ch, 45: 12. Jeremiah, ch, 12: 14–17; ch. 17: 4; ch. 27: 5–7, 11; ch. 28: 14; ch. 30: 3; ch. 32:

6–10, 22, 43, 44. Ezekiel, ch. 20: 6; eh. 44: 28; ch. 45: 1; ch. 48: passim.

Hosea, ch. 2: 8. Habakkuk, ch. 1: 6 l. Zechariah, ch. 10: 1.

Matthew, ch. 5: 45 l; ch. 6: 11, 26, 28, 33; ch. 21: 33; ch. 22: 5; ch. 27: 7. Lukc, ch. 12: 13. John, ch. 4: 5.

Acts, ch. 1: 18; ch. 4: 35, 37; ch. 5: 1, 4; ch. 7: 5, 7, 45; ch. 13: 19; ch. 14: 17; ch. 17: 25–26.

I. Corinthians, ch. 3: 7 l.; ch. 4: 7. II. Corinthians, ch. 9: 10. Hebrews, ch. 2: 7–8; ch. 11: 8, 22.

III.

God's Gifts of Land are Conditional.

Genesis, ch. 1: 28; ch. 2: 15; ch. 3: 17; ch 6: 7, 12–13, 17; ch. 7: 6, 24; ch. 8: 1, 21; ch. 9: 4–6; ch. 14: 20; ch. 28: 22.

Exodus, ch. 9: 26; ch. 13: 5, 11–12; ch. 15: 17; ch. 20: 12; ch. 23: 23–25; ch. 34: 11–14, 26.

Leviticus, ch. 2: 14; ch. 11: passim; ch. 14: 33 ff; ch. 17: 3–4, 10; ch. 18: 3, 24–28; ch. 19: 9–10, 23, 36; ch. 20: 22–25; ch. 23: 10, 22, 39; ch. 25: 2, 10–11, 13, 18, 23, 24, 25, 34; ch. 26: 3–4, 14–16, 31, 35, 39, 43; ch. 27: 30–31.

Numbcrs, ch. 14: 24; ch. 15: 18–19; ch. 18: 13, 24–26; ch. 32: 18, 22, 30, 32; ch. 33: 52–53; ch. 35: 33.

Deuteronomy, ch. 1: 35; ch. 4: 25–27, 37–38; ch. 5: 16; ch. 6: 10–15; ch. 7: 1–2, 12–13; ch. 8: 1, 6–7, 10, 20; ch. 9: 4; ch. 11: 8–10. 13–17, 20–23, 29–31; ch, 12: 1, 10–11, 17–19, 20–21, 29–30; ch. 14: 11–21, 22, 28; ch. 15: 4–5; ch. 17: 2 ff., 14; ch. 18: 1–4, 9; ch. 19: 1–2; ch. 20: 16–17; ch. 21: 1–2, 23; ch. 24: 19–21; ch. 26: 1–2, 10–11, 12; ch. 27: 2–3; ch. 28: 8, 11, 18, 24, etc , 63; ch. 29: 22–28; ch. 30: 1–5, 9, 16, 18, 20.

Joshua—The history of thc conquest of thc land of the Canaanites, whose iniquity was now full, shows that God's land grants are conditional—ch. 6: 17, 26; ch. 14: 9; eh. 20: 2; ch. 23: 12–16.

Judges, eh. 2: 20; eh. 6: 9–10.

I. Kings, ch. 8 : 33–36, 46–51; ch. 9: 8; ch. 14: 15. II. Kings, ch. 15 : 27–28; ch. 16 : 6; ch. 17 : 7–8, 20–23; ch. 18: 11–12; ch. 19: 17; eh. 21 : 11–14; ch. 24: 14; ch. 25 : 11, 21 l., 26

I. Chronicles, ch. 5 : 25–26; ch. 9: 1. II. Chronicles, ch. 6 : 27–31, 36; ch. 7 : 13–14, 19–20; ch. 14 : 7; ch. 30 : 9; ch. 31 : 5–6; ch. 36 : 21.

Ezra, ch. 9: 7, 11, 12 l. Nehemiah, ch. 1 : 8, 9; ch. 9: 37; ch. 10 : 35, 37 l.; ch. 12 : 44 m.; ch. 13 : 12.

Job, ch. 5: 3–5; ch. 28 : 5 f.

Psalms, 25: 13; psm. 37: 2–3; psm. 78: 46–48; psm. 80: 12; psm. 85: 1–2; psm. 95: 11; psm. 105: 44–45; psm. 106: 37–41; psm. 107: 33–34; psm. 111: 5, 6; psm. 135: 12; psm. 136: 21, 22.

Proverbs, ch. 13 : 22; ch. 20 : 21. Ecclesiastes, ch. 5: 9.

Isaiah, ch. 5: 4–6, 8–9; ch. 6 : 11–12; ch. 9: 18–19; ch. 10 : 5–6; ch. 16 : 10; ch. 17 : 9–10; ch. 19 : 6–7; ch. 24 : 1–6; ch. 28 : 24–29; ch. 30 : 22–23; ch. 32 : 13–14; ch. 33 : 8–9; ch. 45 : 18; ch. 47 : 6; ch. 55 : 10; ch. 58 : 13–14.

Jeremiah, ch. 2 : 7, 15; ch. 3 : 1–3; ch. 4: 23–29; ch. 5: 19, 25; ch. 6 : 8; ch. 7 : 12, 20; ch. 8 : 10; ch. 9: 10–13, 16; ch. 11 : 5; ch. 12 : 4, 7, 10–11; ch. 14 : 2–6; ch. 16 : 13, 18; ch. 18 : 7–10, 16; ch. 22 : 6–9; ch. 22 : 26; ch. 23 : 10; ch. 26 : 4–6, 18; ch. 32 : 23–24; ch. 35 : 15; ch. 40 : 3; ch. 48 : 8–9, 21, 33; ch. 49 : 2, 10, 13, 27, 30, 36; ch. 50 : 13, 19, 22; ch. 51 : 37, 43, 62; ch. 52 : 27.

Lamentations, ch. 1 : 1; ch. 4 : 9; ch. 5 : 18. The whole book is a commentary on the truth that land is forfeited through sin.

Ezekiel ch. 5 : 5–12; ch. 6 : 1–8; eh. 7 : 24; ch. 11 : 15–16; ch. 12 : 14, 19–20; ch. 14 : 12–13 ff.; ch. 16 : 48–52; ch. 20 : 15–16, 28, 38, 40, 42; ch. 22: 24; ch. 25 : 10; eh. 26 : 5, 14; ch. 29 : 3, 9–11; ch. 30 : 12; ch. 32 : 15; ch. 33 : 25–29; ch. 35 : 3–9; ch. 36 : 16–19; ch. 29 : 33.

Daniel, ch. 9 : 7, 11. Hosea, ch. 2 : 8–12; ch. 4 : 1–3; ch. 8 : 7; ch 10 : 8. Joel, ch. 2 : 3. Amos, ch. 1 : 4, 8, 12, 15; ch. 2 : 2, 5, 9, 10; ch. 4 : 7, 9; ch. 5 : 2, 11, 27; ch. 7 : 17. Micah ch. 2 : 1-4; ch. 3 : 12; ch. 5 : 11; ch. 6 : 16; ch. 7 : 13. Zephaniah, ch 1 : 18; ch. 2 : 9;

eh. 3: 6. Haggai, ch. 1:9–11; ch. 2:17. Zechariah, ch. 5: 1–4; ch. 7: 14; ch. 14: 17. Malachi, ch. 1: 3; ch. 2: 15 m; ch. 3: 8–11.

Matthew, ch. 22: 21; ch. 23: 23 f.; ch. 25: 14–30. Mark, ch. 12: 1–9. Luke, ch. 13: 6–9; ch. 19: 12–27; ch. 20: 9–16.

Hebrews, ch. 7: 2, 4–9.

IV.

The Future of Earth.

Genesis. ch. 1: 28. Exodus, ch. 20:12. Deuteronomy, ch. 5: 16–33; ch. 30: 1–5.

II. Kings, ch. 21: 7–8. I. Chronicles, ch. 16: 15–18; ch. 17: 9; ch. 22: 25.

Psalm, 2: 6, 9; psm. 9: 6–7; psm. 15: passim; psm. 19: 1–4; psm, 22: 26–27; psm. 24: 3–7; psm. 25: 13; psm. 27: 13; psm. 34: 11–13, 16; psm. 37: 9, 11, 18, 22, 27, 29, 34; psm. 41: 2 f.; psm. 46: 5, 10; psm. 48: 8 l.; psm. 69: 35–36; psm. 72: 3, 7–11; psm. 78: 69; psm. 92: 13; psm. 96: 1, 12–13; psm. 97: 1; psm. 98: 4, 8–9; psm. 100: 1; psm. 101: 6, 8; psm. 102: 25, 26; psm. 104: 5; psm. 125: 1–2; psm. 145: 10 f.; psm. 146: 10; psm. 147: 6; psm. 148; 3–10.

Proverbs, ch. 2: 21, 22; ch. 10: 30; ch. 11: 31; ch. 12: 3, 7.

Isaiah, ch. 2: 2–4; ch. 4: 5; ch. 11: 6–9, 12, 14–16; ch. 12: 5; ch. 14: 1; ch. 25: 6; ch. 26: 1; ch. 27: 6; ch. 32: 15–18; ch. 33: 20–21; ch. 35: 1, 7–10; ch. 40: 4–5: ch. 41: 18–19; ch. 42: 4, 10–12; ch. 44: 23; ch. 45: 8, 22; ch. 49: 8–13, 22–23; ch. 51: 6–7; ch. 55: 12–13; ch. 59: 19; ch. 60: 13–21; ch. 61: 7; ch. 65: 17–25; ch. 66: 22.

Jeremiah, ch. 3: 16–19; ch. 12: 15; ch. 16: 15; ch. 17: 25; ch. 23: 5–8; ch. 30: 3; ch. 31: 3–4, 10, 31–40; ch. 32: 37–42; eh. 33: 9, 15; ch. 48: 47; eh. 49: 6, 33, 39.

Lamentations, ch. 3: 31–33.

Ezekiel, ch. 11: 17–21; ch. 20: 40; ch. 28: 25–26; ch. 34: 23–31; ch. 35: 14–15; ch. 36: 8–15, 24–35; ch. 37:

12–14, 21–28; ch. 38: 8; ch. 39: 25–29. Chapters 40–48 contain the vision of the new temple. They are perhaps the most obscure portion of Scripture. None can fully understand them now; but their meaning will be clear to those living in the "new earth."—ch. 43: 7.

Hosea, ch. 1: 10; ch. 2: 18–23; ch. 3: 5. Joel, ch. 2: 18-27; ch. 3: 1–2, 17–21. Amos, ch. 9: 11–15. Micah, ch. 4: 1–4. Nahum, ch. 1: 15; ch. 2: 2. Habakkuk, ch. 2: 14. Zechariah, ch. 2: 4–5, 12; ch. 3: 9 l.; ch. 8: 3, 8, 12; ch. 9: 10, 16; ch. 10: 10; ch. 12: 6; ch. 13: 2; ch. 14: 9, 14, 16.

Matthew, ch. 5: 5, 18; ch. 6: 10; ch. 13: 41, 49–50; ch. 19: 28–29; ch. 23: 39; ch. 24: 30 l., 37–51; ch. 25: 31, 41; ch. 26: 64 l.; ch. 28: 30 l. Mark, ch. 13: 26, 31. Luke ch. 2: 14 l.; ch. 3: 5–6; ch. 22: 29–30; ch. 23: 30. John, ch. 1: 29; ch. 3: 35; ch. 12: 47. Acts, ch. 15: 16–17.

Romans, ch. 5: 20; ch. 8: 19–21; ch 11: 13–24. I. Corinthians, ch. 15: 20–22, 45, 52 l. II. Corinthians, ch. 5: 17, 19. Galatians, ch. 3: 15–19. Ephesians, ch. 1: 22. Colossians, ch. 1: 20. Hebrews, ch. 1: 11–12; ch. 2: 8; ch. 4: 1, 8, 9, (cf. v. 4); ch. 8: 10–11; ch. 12: 26. II. Peter, ch. 3: 1–13. Jude, ch. 14.

Revelations, ch. 2: 7, 26; ch. 3: 12; ch. 6: 13–17; ch. 7: 2–9, 15–17; ch. 14: 1, 16; ch. 15: 4; ch. 20: 11; ch. 21: 1, 2, 5, 8, 10; ch. 22: 2.

OMISSIONS.

On page 30, among the features of a primitive industrial condition there should have been mentioned the absence of crime against property. Larceny, burglary, forgery, and other like crimes are as infrequent as bolts, locks and safes.

The phrase, "tenants at will," near the top of page 80, should have been explained. The meaning of the phrase is that the rigorous exaction of a rent tax will make the tenure of many land-owners uncertain and precarious.

There are apparent contradictions between statements on page 98 and pages 106 and 111; and between page 110 (top) and page 152. These verbal inconsistencies will not, it is thought, perplex the careful and intelligent reader. They will delight the captious reader. But the critical reader may be helped by them. The author's only apology is that he did not see the sheets before they went to press, and failed to notice in the manuscript that the statements were not properly qualified.

The implication that the pyramids of Egypt were built after the days of Joseph, was also unnoticed till it was too late to correct it.

On page 212, the tax on succession, on bequests and legacies, should have been enumerated among the direct taxes. It is a direct tax and cannot be shifted. It is a tax on ability and not on necessity. It was inadvertently omitted in copying.

Lightning Source UK Ltd.
Milton Keynes UK
UKHW032253141118
332327UK00005B/232/P